OLYMPIAD WORKBOOK

NATIONAL SCIENCE OLYMPIAD

01 **Learning Objectives**

02 **Multiple Choice Questions**

03 **HOTS (Achievers Section)**

04 **Model Test Paper**

05 **Answer Keys and Solutions**

06 **OMR Answer Sheet**

Published by:

V&S PUBLISHERS

F-2/16, Ansari road, Daryaganj, New Delhi-110002
☎ 23240026, 23240027 • *Fax:* 011-23240028
✉ info@vspublishers.com • ⊕ www.vspublishers.com

Online Brandstore: amazon.in/vspublishers

Regional Office : Hyderabad
5-1-707/1, Brij Bhawan (Beside Central Bank of India Lane)
Bank Street, Koti, Hyderabad - 500 095
☎ 040-24737290
✉ vspublishershyd@gmail.com

Follow us on:   

BUY OUR BOOKS FROM: AMAZON   FLIPKART

© **Copyright:** *V&S PUBLISHERS*
ISBN 978-81-977761-1-3
New Edition

PUBLISHER'S NOTE

V&S Publishers has carved a significant niche in the publishing industry over the last decade, having successfully published more than 1000 titles across 9 languages spanning over 50 subject categories. Being known for the quality of content, we have built a reputation of excellence and reliability. We have consistently delivered **"Value & Substance"** to our readers, through a wide range of titles across a variety of genres covering school books, fiction and non-fiction that caters to different people from every section of the society.

The **Olympiad Guidebooks for classes 1-10** across all subjects, launched almost a decade ago, under the **GEN X Imprint**, became a go-to-source for the school students in no time, owing to their invaluable and substantive content written in a guidebook pattern,.

Having successfully sold a million copies of the same and in response to demand by both students as well as shopkeepers nationwide; we now present before you our newly launched **Olympiad Workbook Series**, designed for **classes 1-10 across 4 subjects**.

The workbooks are meticulously curated by a team of experienced educators, researchers and subject matter experts, edited by professionals and peer reviewed by teachers. The team has poured its efforts and expertise into creating a crisp and concise workbook which will help and guide the students to the path of success in Olympiad exams. The **MCQs** identified will not only help in scoring top marks in Olympiads but also inculcate a sense of deeper understanding of the subject, by way of solving **HOTS** and referring to complete solutions at the end of the book.

Here we present our new release– **OLYMPIAD WORKBOOK (NSO) CLASS–9** having following features:

- Based on the latest syllabi
- MCQs with comprehensive coverage of topics
- HOTS Questions liberally included
- A dedicated chapter on logical reasoning
- Model test paper for thorough practice
- Sample OMR sheet for real time simulation

We have made sure through our best efforts, that this workbook strictly follows the latest syllabi and patterns of the Olympiad Examination.

As **V&S Publishers** continuously strive to enhance the readability and maintain the credibility of our academic publications, we seek the support of our valuable readers in influencing and enriching the lives of future generations of students.

P.S. While every care has been taken to ensure the correctness of the content, if you come across any error, howsoever minor, do not hesitate to discuss with teachers while pointing that out to us in no uncertain terms.

We wish you all the best for your exams!

DISTINCTIVE FEATURES

01

Learning Objectives

They list the whole chapter as subtopics, helping the teachers to guide children in a step-by-step manner.

02

Multiple Choice Questions

MCQs act as an excellent learning aid, helping you to understand and work on your mistakes.

03

HOTS (Achievers Section)

The High Order Thinking Questions aim to help the student to solve Application-based questions and gain practical understanding of the subject.

04

Model Test Paper

Model test paper are provided at the end of each book, which help the student to test the knowledge which they have gained after thorough reading of all chapters.

05

Answer Key

Detailed Answer Key along with explanations aid the pupil to indentify, understand the mistakes they make during the course of Olympiad preparation.

CONTENTS

MATTER IN OUR SURROUNDINGS

LEARNING OBJECTIVES

➤ Characteristics of particles of matter
➤ Solid, liquid and gas matter

➤ The process of evaporation
➤ Factors affecting evaporation

MULTIPLE CHOICE QUESTIONS

1. Helium gas is a matter because __________.
   (A) It has mass and occupies volume
   (B) It has no definite volume
   (C) It can be compressed easily
   (D) It has a mass

2. Which of the following is correct arrangement of decreasing order of force of attraction between particles?
   (A) Water, air, chalk
   (B) Sugar, alcohol, nitrogen
   (C) Sulphur dioxide, carbon disulphide, sulphur
   (D) Oxygen, water sugar

3. On converting 0°C, –6°C, 273°C into Kelvin, the correct sequence of temperature will be __________.
   (A) 273 K, 267 K, 546 K
   (B) 273 K, 279 K, 546 K
   (C) 273 K, 267 K, 0 K
   (D) –273 K, –279 K, 0 K

4. For any substance the temperature remains same during the change of state due to __________.
   (A) Loss of heat
   (B) Latent heat
   (C) Less supply of heat
   (D) Lattice energy

5. What will be boiling point of water at hill station?
   (A) 100°C
   (B) <100°C
   (C) >100°C
   (D) Either less than 100°C

6. The mixture of sulphur and sodium chloride can be separated by __________.
   (A) Dissolving in water followed by filtration and evaporation
   (B) Sublimation
   (C) Dissolving in alcohol followed by filtration
   (D) Crystallization

7. Which one of the following statement is correct in respect of fluids?
   (A) Only gases behave as fluids
   (B) Only liquids are fluids
   (C) Gases and solids behave as fluids
   (D) Gases and liquids behave as fluids

8. When we determine the boiling point of liquid, the thermometer _________.
   (A) Should dip into liquid
   (B) Should be above the liquid and remain vertical
   (C) Should touch the bottom of container
   (D) Should be placed slanting in the liquid

9. Which of the following statements is incorrect?
   (A) The particles of matter are very-very small
   (B) The particles of matter attract one another
   (C) The particles of all the matter have spaces between them
   (D) The particles of some of the matter are moving constantly

10. The best evidence for the existence and movement of particles in liquids was provided by _________.
    (A) Kerosene   (B) Krypton
    (C) Carbon steel   (D) Carbon dioxide

11. During respiration, glucose and oxygen enter our body cells whereas waste products like carbon dioxide and water leave body cells by the process of _________.
    (A) Osmosis   (B) Effusion
    (C) Diffusion   (D) Plasmolysis

12. Which of the following energy is absorbed during the change of state of a substance?
    (A) Heat capacity   (B) Latent heat
    (C) Heat of solution (D) Specific heat

13. On converting 308 K, 329 K and 391 K to Celsius scale, the correct sequence of temperature will be _________.
    (A) 33°C, 56°C and 118°C
    (B) 35°C, 56°C and 118°C
    (C) 35°C, 56°C and 119°C
    (D) 56°C, 119°C and 35°C

14. Which of the following are also considered to be the states of matter?
    (i) BEC (ii) BHC (iii) plasma (iv) platelets
    (A) (i) and (ii)   (B) (i) and (iii)
    (C) (ii) and (iii)   (D) (iii) and (iv)

15. If the temperature of an object is 268 K, it will be equivalent to _________.
    (A) –5°C   (B) +5°C
    (C) –25°C   (D) 368°C

16. The boiling point of ethane is, –88°C. This temperature will be equivalent to _________.
    (A) 185 K   (B) 361 K
    (C) 288 K   (D) 285 K

17. When heat is constantly supplied by a burner to boiling water, then the temperature of water during vaporisation _________.
    (A) Rises very slowly
    (B) First rises and then becomes constant
    (C) Rises rapidly until steam is produced
    (D) Does not rise at all

18. When water at 0°C freezes to form ice at the same temperature of 0°C, then it _________.
    (A) Absorbs some heat
    (B) Release some heat
    (C) Neither absorbs nor releases heat
    (D) Absorbs exactly 3.34×105 j/kg of heat

19. In the following diagram ammonia gas obtained from ammonium hydroxide reacts with HCl (g) obtained from hydrochloric acid, and form white fumes of ammonium chloride. Observe the following diagram and choose the correct option.

Cotton dipped in ammonium hydroxide

Cotton dipped in hydrochloric acid

(A) White fumes ring will be formed at the centre

(B) White fumes ring will be formed near 2nd end

(C) White fumes ring will be formed near 1st end

(D) White fumes ring will not be formed at all

20. During summer days water kept in an earthen pot (pitcher) becomes cool because of the phenomenon of _________.

(A) Osmosis

(B) Evaporation

(C) Transpiration

(D) Diffusion

21. The evaporation of water increases under the following conditions _________.

(A) Increase in surface area, decrease in temperature

(B) Increase in surface area, rise in temperature

(C) Increase in temperature, decrease in surface area

(D) Increase in temperature, increase in surface area addition of common salt

22. One of the following does not undergo sublimation. This one is _________.

(A) Iodine

(B) Camphor

(C) Sodium chloride

(D) Ammonium chloride

23. When a gas jar full of air is placed upside down on a gas jar full of bromine vapours, the red – brown vapours of bromine from the lower jar go upward into the jar containing air. In this experiment _________.

(A) Bromine is heavier than air

(B) Air is heavier than bromine

(C) Coth air and bromine have the same density

(D) Bromine cannot be heavier than air because it is going upwards against gravity

24. Ice floats on water because _________.

(A) It is solid

(B) It is low melting solid

(C) It has higher density than water

(D) It has lower density than water due to more volume

25. Seema took a 100 ml beaker and filled half the beaker with water and marked the level of water. She dissolved some salt with the help of a glass rod and recorded water level again. Choose the correct observation related to above activity.

(A) The water level decreases

(B) There is little increase in water level

(C) The water level remains the same

(D) The water level increases appreciably

26. Which of the following has minimum kinetic energy?

(A) Particles of ice below 0°

(B) Particles of water at 0°

(C) Particles of water at 100°

(D) Particles of steam at 100°

27. Which one of the following statements is not true?

(A) The molecules in a gas exert negligibly small forces on each other, except during collisions

(B) The molecules of a gas occupy all the space available

(C) The molecules in a liquid are arranged in a regular pattern

(D) The molecules in a solid vibrate about a fixed position

28. Convert the temperature of 300 K to the Celsius scale.

(A) 30°C

(B) 27°C

(C) 28°C

(D) 26°C

29. Which of the following process/processes release heat?
   (i) Condensation   (ii) Vaporisation
   (iii) Freezing   (iv) Melting
   (A) (i) and (ii)   (B) (i) and (iii)
   (C) only (ii)   (D) Only (iv)

30. Particles of matter are ________.
   (A) Stationary
   (B) In continuous motion
   (C) Rotating about on axis
   (D) Vibrating in one position

HOTS (ACHIEVERS SECTION)

31. Which of the following is not true?
   (i) On increasing the temperature of solids, the force of attraction between particles increases
   (ii) On increasing the temperature of solids, kinetic energy of particles will decrease
   (iii) Melting point is the temperature, at which a solid melts to become a liquid at the atmospheric pressure
   (A) Only (i)   (B) (i) and (ii)
   (C) (i), (ii) and (iii)   (D) None of these

32. Find the increase in the temperature of 1kg of water if 1000 J of heat is supplied to it.
   (A) $\left(\dfrac{4186}{1000}\right)^{°C}$ (B) $\left(\dfrac{1000}{4186}\right)^{°C}$
   (C) $(1000 \times 4186)°C$ (D) $(4186 - 1000)°C$

33. It was observed during a hail storm that ice balls turned into water when they reached the ground. At what height could the rain drops have formed into ice balls? Assume that g is 10 ms^{-2}
   (A) 320 km   (B) 350 km
   (C) 334 km   (D) 343 km

34. The temperature of 104°F when measured on a Kelvin scale will give the reading of ________.
   (A) 313 K   (B) 302 K
   (C) 307 K   (D) 380 K

35. What is mean by sublimation?
   (A) change of state directly from solid to liquid without changing into gas state
   (B) change of state directly from soil to gas without changing into liquid state
   (C) change of state directly from solid to gas without changing into ice state
   (D) change of state directly from solid to gas without changing into liquid state

⏱ ⏱ ⏱

Darken Your Choice with HB Pencil

1.	Ⓐ Ⓑ Ⓒ Ⓓ	8.	Ⓐ Ⓑ Ⓒ Ⓓ	15.	Ⓐ Ⓑ Ⓒ Ⓓ	22	Ⓐ Ⓑ Ⓒ Ⓓ	29.	Ⓐ Ⓑ Ⓒ Ⓓ
2.	Ⓐ Ⓑ Ⓒ Ⓓ	9.	Ⓐ Ⓑ Ⓒ Ⓓ	16.	Ⓐ Ⓑ Ⓒ Ⓓ	23.	Ⓐ Ⓑ Ⓒ Ⓓ	30.	Ⓐ Ⓑ Ⓒ Ⓓ
3.	Ⓐ Ⓑ Ⓒ Ⓓ	10.	Ⓐ Ⓑ Ⓒ Ⓓ	17.	Ⓐ Ⓑ Ⓒ Ⓓ	24.	Ⓐ Ⓑ Ⓒ Ⓓ	31.	Ⓐ Ⓑ Ⓒ Ⓓ
4.	Ⓐ Ⓑ Ⓒ Ⓓ	11.	Ⓐ Ⓑ Ⓒ Ⓓ	18.	Ⓐ Ⓑ Ⓒ Ⓓ	25.	Ⓐ Ⓑ Ⓒ Ⓓ	32.	Ⓐ Ⓑ Ⓒ Ⓓ
5.	Ⓐ Ⓑ Ⓒ Ⓓ	12.	Ⓐ Ⓑ Ⓒ Ⓓ	19.	Ⓐ Ⓑ Ⓒ Ⓓ	26.	Ⓐ Ⓑ Ⓒ Ⓓ	33.	Ⓐ Ⓑ Ⓒ Ⓓ
6.	Ⓐ Ⓑ Ⓒ Ⓓ	13.	Ⓐ Ⓑ Ⓒ Ⓓ	20.	Ⓐ Ⓑ Ⓒ Ⓓ	27.	Ⓐ Ⓑ Ⓒ Ⓓ	34.	Ⓐ Ⓑ Ⓒ Ⓓ
7.	Ⓐ Ⓑ Ⓒ Ⓓ	14.	Ⓐ Ⓑ Ⓒ Ⓓ	21.	Ⓐ Ⓑ Ⓒ Ⓓ	28.	Ⓐ Ⓑ Ⓒ Ⓓ	35.	Ⓐ Ⓑ Ⓒ Ⓓ

IS MATTER AROUND US PURE?

LEARNING OBJECTIVES

➤ Different types of elements
➤ Solutions, colloids and suspensions
➤ Separation of components of a mixture

MULTIPLE CHOICE QUESTIONS

1. Which of the following is not an element?
   (A) Germanium   (B) Silica
   (C) Carbon   (D) Silicon

2. Which of the following are compounds?
   (i) CO   (ii) No
   (iii) NO   (iv) Co
   (A) (i) and (ii)   (B) (i) and (iii)
   (C) (ii) and (iii) (D) (ii) and (iv)

3. Identify the pure substance from the given material __________.
   (A) Calcium oxide (B) Wood
   (C) Air   (D) All of these

4. One of the following substances is neither a good conductor of electricity nor an insulator. This substance is __________.
   (A) Chromium   (B) Gallium
   (C) Germanium   (D) Potassium

5. Which of the following is not a mixture?
   (A) Kerosene   (B) Alcohol
   (C) Air   (D) Petrol

6. Which of the following statements are true for pure substances?
   (i) Pure substances contain only one kind of particles
   (ii) Pure substances may be compounds or mixture
   (iii) Pure substances have the same composition throughout
   (iv) Pure substances can be exemplified by all elements other than nickel
   (A) (i) and (ii)   (B) (ii) and (iii)
   (C) (i) and (iii)   (D) (ii) and (iv)

7. Which of the following does not have a fixed melting point/boiling point?
   (A) Ethanol   (B) Air
   (C) Oxygen   (D) Gold

8. If 10 g of sodium hydroxide is dissolved in 150 g of water, then calculate the mass percent of sodium hydroxide in the solution __________.
   (A) 8.2%   (B) 6.25%
   (C) 5%   (D) 7.5%

9. Which of the following is homogeneous in nature?
   (i) Ice   (ii) Wood
   (iii) Soil   (iv) Air
   (A) (i) and (ii)   (B) (i) and (iv)
   (C) (ii) and (iii) (D) (iii) and (iv)

10. If 110 g of copper sulphate is present in 550 g of solution, what will be the concentration of solution?
    (A) 11%   (B) 20%
    (C) 55%   (D) 22%

11. Milk of magnesia is __________.
   (A) A true solution
   (B) A colloid
   (C) A suspension
   (D) A homogeneous mixture

12. Which one of the following liquids will leave behind a residue on heating?
   (A) Brine   (B) Mercury
   (C) Bromine   (D) Alcohol

13. Which one of the following is most likely to exhibit Tyndall effect?
   (A) Chalk powder and water mixture
   (B) Potash alum and water mixture
   (C) Sugar and water mixture
   (D) Potassium permanganate and water mixture

14. Which one of the following is a solid foam __________.
   (A) Ruby   (B) Shaving cream
   (C) Bread   (D) Butter

15. Which one of the following will show the properties of electrophoresis?
   (A) Hydrosols
   (B) Carbondioxide
   (C) Chalk in water
   (D) Arseneous sulphide

16. Which of the following is not an emulsion?
   (A) Butter   (B) Milk
   (C) Shaving cream (D) Face cream

17. One of the following represents the solution of solid in a solid. This one is __________.
   (A) Boron   (B) Brass
   (C) Bread   (D) Beryllium

18. Which one of the following is an aerosol?
   (A) Mist   (B) Sugar solution
   (C) Egg yolk   (D) Vapour

19. A solution is prepared by dissolving 80 g of salt in 500 g of water. Find the concentration of the solution.
   (A) 10%   (B) 11%
   (C) 13.8%   (D) 1.38%

20. Which of the following are physical changes?
   (i)   Melting of iron metal
   (ii) Rusting of iron metal
   (iii) Bending of iron rod
   (iv) Drawing a wire of iron metal
   (A) (i), (ii) and (iii)   (B) (i), (iii) and (iv)
   (C) (i), (ii) and (iv)   (D) (ii), (iii) and (iv)

21. Tincture of iodine has antiseptic properties. This solution is made by dissolving __________.
   (A) Iodine in alcohol
   (B) Iodine in acetone
   (C) Iodine in water
   (D) Iodine in potassium iodide

22. A mixture of sulphur and carbon disulphide is __________.
   (A) Heterogeneous and shows tyndall effect
   (B) Heterogeneous and does not show tyndall effect
   (C) Heterogeneous and shows tyndall effect
   (D) Heterogeneous and does not show tyndall effect

23. Which of the following are chemical changes?
   (i)   Decaying of wood
   (ii) Burning of wood
   (iii) Sawing of wood
   (iv) Hammering of nail into wood
   (A) (i) and (ii)   (B) (ii) and (iii)
   (C) (i) and (iv)   (D) (ii) and (iv)

24. A mixture of milk and ground oil can be separated by __________.
   (A) Sublimation
   (B) Separating funnel
   (C) Filtration
   (D) Evaporation

25. Which one of the following pair of gases cannot be separated by diffusion method?

(A) CO_2 and NO_2 (B) CO_2 and N_2O_2
(C) CO_2 and H_2 (D) CO_2 and N_2O

26. For removing the greasy spot from the shirt what method should we use?
    (A) Sublimation
    (B) Using suitable solvent
    (C) Evaporation
    (D) Solvent extraction

27. Naphthalene can be separated from sand __________.
    (A) By sublimation
    (B) By crystallisation
    (C) By distillation
    (D) Using suitable solvent

28. A solution contains 50 ml of alcohol mixed with 150 ml of water. Calculate the concentration of this solution __________.

(A) 15%   (B) 10%
(C) 25%   (D) 20%

29. Name the metal which is found in liquid form.
    (A) Antimony   (B) Tin
    (C) Bromine   (D) Mercury

30. The rusting of an iron object is called __________.
    (A) Corrosion and it is a chemical change
    (B) Corrosion and it is a physical as well as chemical change
    (C) Dissolution and it is a chemical change
    (D) Dissolution and it is a physical change

HOTS (ACHIEVERS SECTION)

31. Which of the following is not false?
    (i) Compounds are homogeneous substance.
    (ii) The composition of a compound is fixed, the constituents are present in a fixed proportion by mass.
    (iii) A compound cannot be separated into its components by physical methods.
    (A) Only (i)
    (B) (i) and (ii)
    (C) (i), (ii) and (iii)
    (D) None of these

32. Technical names of some colloids are given under column I whereas the dispersion media are under column II. Match column I with column II and choose the correct option.

Column I	Column II
(A) Aerosol	(i) Solid
(B) Emulsion	(ii) Liquid
(C) Solid Foam	(iii) Gas

    (A) (A) (i), (B) (ii), (C) (iii)
    (B) (A) (ii), (B) (iii), (C) (i)
    (C) (A) (iii), (B) (ii), (C) (i)
    (D) (A) (i), (B) (iii), (C) (ii)

33. The empirical formula of a compound is CH_2O. Its molecular weight is 90. The molecular formula of the compound is (Atomic weight of $C = 12$, $H = 1$, and $O = 16$)?
    (A) $C_3H_7O_3$
    (B) $C_3H_6O_3$
    (C) $C_3H_4O_7$
    (D) $C_2H_4O_2$

Direction (34–35): The figure given below is showing separation of ammonium chloride and salt by sublimation. Referring to this diagram, answer the questions given below:

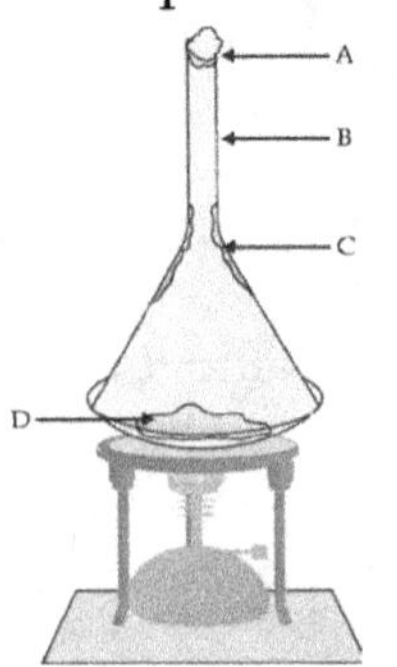
A
B
C
D

34. Which of the following is the mixture of ammonium chloride and salt?
    (A) A   (B) B
    (C) C   (D) D

35. Which of the following is showing the solidified ammonium chloride after separation?
    (A) A   (B) B
    (C) C   (D) D

ATOMS AND MOLECULES

➤ The laws of chemical combination
➤ Dalton's Atomic Theory
➤ The concept of molecules and chemical formulae

MULTIPLE CHOICE QUESTIONS

1. Certain mass of carbon burns with a given mass of oxygen to form certain mass of carbon dioxide, which law of chemical combinations is used in this process of formation of compound?
   (A) Law of conservation of mass
   (B) Law of constant proportion
   (C) Law of multiple proportion
   (D) Gay Lussac's law

2. The atomic theory of matter was proposed by __________.
   (A) Lavoisier
   (B) Proust
   (C) John Dalton
   (D) John Kennedy

3. Which postulates of Dalton's atomic theory gives laws of conservation of mass?
   (A) Atom can neither be created nor be destroyed
   (B) Atoms of same elements are similar
   (C) Atoms of different elements are different
   (D) Atom combine in fixed ratio to form compound

4. The atoms of which of the following pairs of elements are most likely to exist in free state?
   (A) Hydrogen and helium
   (B) Helium and neon
   (C) Argon and carbon
   (D) Neon and nitrogen

5. Which of the following elements has the same molecular mass as its atomic mass?
   (A) Nitrogen
   (B) Oxygen
   (C) Neon
   (D) Chlorine

6. In water, hydrogen and oxygen are present in the ratio of __________.
   (A) $1:2$
   (B) $1:8$
   (C) $2:12$
   (D) $2:3$

7. What is the mass of 0.2 mole of lead nitrate? ($N = 14$, $O = 16$, $Pb = 207$)
   (A) 33.1 g
   (B) 3.31 g
   (C) 66.2 g
   (D) 6.62 g

8. Find the total percentage of oxygen in magnesium nitrate crystal i.e., $Mg(NO_3)_2 \cdot 6H_2O$ (Atomic weight: $H=1$, $N=14$, $O=16$, $Mg=24$)
   (A) 60%
   (B) 65%
   (C) 70%
   (D) 75%

9. Kalium is the Latin name of __________.
   (A) Krypton
   (B) Potassium
   (C) Calcium
   (D) Phosphorus

10. The atomic number of an element X is 13. What will be the number of electrons in its ion X^{3+}?

(A) 11   (B) 16

(C) 15   (D) 10

11. The anion of an element has __________.

(A) Less electrons than the normal atom

(B) More electrons than the normal atom

(C) More protons than the normal atom

(D) Same number of electrons as normal atom

12. The smallest particle of a substance that is capable of independent existence is __________.

(A) Electron

(B) Proton

(C) Atom

(D) Molecule

13. If the number of electrons in an ion Z^{3-} is 10, the atomic number of element Z will be __________.

(A) 7   (B) 5

(C) 10   (D) 8

14. How many litres of ammonia are present in 3.4 kg of it? (N = 14, H = 1)?

(A) 22.4 litres

(B) 44.8 litres

(C) 4480 litres

(D) 2240 litres

15. Two elements X and Y have valencies of 5 and 3, & 3 and 2, respectively. The elements X and Y are most likely to be __________ respectively.

(A) Sulphur and iron

(B) Nitrogen and iron

(C) Phosphorus and nitrogen

(D) Copper and sulphur

16. The cation of an element has __________.

(A) Less electrons than a neutral atom

(B) Less protons than a neutral atom

(C) More electrons than a neutral atom

(D) The same number of electrons as its neutral atom

17. A particle P has 18 electrons, 20 neutrons and 19 protons. This particle must be __________.

(A) A molecule

(B) A cation

(C) An anion

(D) A binary compound

18. Molecular compounds are usually formed by combination between __________.

(A) Two different metals

(B) Two different non-metals

(C) Two gaseous elements

(D) A metal and a non-metal

19. The formula of a compound is X_3Y. The valencies of elements X and Y will be, __________ respectively.

(A) 1 and 3   (B) 3 and 1

(C) 2 and 3   (D) 3 and 2

20. What will be the mass of 1 mole of $FeSO_4 \cdot 7H_2O$?

(A) 585 g

(B) 278 g

(C) 287 g

(D) 270 g

21. What will be the formula mass of $CaCl_2$ (Ca = 40, Cl = 3.5)?

(A) 99 amu

(B) 100 amu

(C) 111 amu

(D) 122 amu

22. The mass of a single atom of an element Z is 2.65×10^{-23} g. What is its gram atomic mass?

(A) 1.569 g

(B) 15.69 g

(C) 156.9 g

(D) 15.69 mg

23. In $_8O^{16}$, the number 16 stands for
    ___________.

    (A) Atomic number
    (B) Atomic mass
    (C) Atomic mass scale
    (D) Number of electrons

24. All samples of carbon dioxide contain carbon and oxygen in the mass ratio of $3 : 8$. This is in agreement with the law of ___________.

    (A) Conservation of mass
    (B) Constant proportion
    (C) Multiple proportion
    (D) Reciprocal proportion

25. The best standard for atomic mass is _____.

    (A) O – 16   (B) S – 32
    (C) C – 12   (D) H – 1

26. Modern atomic symbol was proposed by ___________.

    (A) Berzelius   (B) Dalton
    (C) Bohr   (D) A. Lavosier

27. How many moles are present in 12.044×10^{22} molecules of sulphur dioxide?

    (A) 0.1 mole   (B) 0.2 mole
    (C) 0.3 mole   (D) 0.4 mole

28. A compound has the following percentage composition (H = 2.04%, S = 32.65%, O = 65.31%. Relative molecular mass of compound = 98. What will be its molecular formula (H = 1, S = 32, O = 16)?

    (A) HSO_4
    (B) $H(SP_4)_2$
    (C) $H_2(SO_4)_3$
    (D) H_2SO_4

29. The symbol of a metal element which is used in making thermometers is ___________.

    (A) Mg   (B) Sg
    (C) Hg   (D) Ag

30. What will be the atoms in 0.2 mole of sodium (Na)?

    (A) 12.044×10^{22} atoms
    (B) 6.022×10^{23} atoms
    (C) 12.044×10^{23} atoms
    (D) 1.2044×10^{22} atoms

HOTS (ACHIEVERS SECTION)

31. Which of the following is/are true?
    (i) The chemical formula of a molecular compound is determined by atomic number of each element.
    (ii) An atom is the smallest particle of elements.
    (iii) Molecules are the smallest particle of the substance, element or compound which can exist in free state under ordinary condition.

    (A) Only (i)
    (B) (i) and (ii)
    (C) (ii) and (iii)
    (D) (i), (ii) and (iii)

32. The weight of 0.885 moles of $Mg(NO_3)_2$ is ___________.

    (A) 131 g   (B) 13.1 g
    (C) 85.5 g   (D) 1.31 g

33. Eutrophication is the process in which dissolved oxygen in water is reduced due to excessive growth of algae. This is the result of ___________.

    (A) Change in temperature of water
    (B) Extra loading of nutrients in water body
    (C) Stratification of aquatic habitat
    (D) Bioaccumulation in algae

34. Find the number of iron atoms in a piece of iron weighing 2.8 g (Atomic mass of iron = 56).
   (A) 3.011×10^{22} atoms
   (B) 3.11×10^{23} atoms
   (C) 3.10×10^{23} atoms
   (D) 30.1×10^{21} atoms

35. Bohr's model can explain ____________.
   (A) Spectrum of hydrogen molecule
   (B) Spectrum of hydrogen atom
   (C) Spectrum of any atom or ion having one electron only
   (D) Solar spectrum

Darken Your Choice with HB Pencil

1.	A B C D	8.	A B C D	15.	A B C D	22	A B C D	29.	A B C D
2.	A B C D	9.	A B C D	16.	A B C D	23.	A B C D	30.	A B C D
3.	A B C D	10.	A B C D	17.	A B C D	24.	A B C D	31.	A B C D
4.	A B C D	11.	A B C D	18.	A B C D	25.	A B C D	32.	A B C D
5.	A B C D	12.	A B C D	19.	A B C D	26.	A B C D	33.	A B C D
6.	A B C D	13.	A B C D	20.	A B C D	27.	A B C D	34.	A B C D
7.	A B C D	14.	A B C D	21.	A B C D	28.	A B C D	35.	A B C D

OLYMPIAD WORKBOOK (NSO) CLASS – 9

STRUCTURE OF ATOM 

➤ The structure of atom
➤ The contribution of Thomson, Rutherford and Bohr
➤ Practical applications of isotopes

MULTIPLE CHOICE QUESTIONS

1. The first model of an atom was given by __________.
   (A) Eugen Goldstein
   (B) J.J. Thomson
   (C) Neils Bohr
   (D) Ernest Rutherford

2. What are cathode rays?
   (A) Positively charged
   (B) Negatively charged
   (C) Neutral
   (D) All of these

3. Which of the following statements is always correct?
   (A) an atom has equal number of electrons, protons and neutrons
   (B) an atom has equal number of neutrons
   (C) an atom has equal number of electrons and neutrons
   (D) an atom has equal number of electrons and protons

4. Rutherford's alpha particle scattering experiment led to the discovery of __________.
   (A) Electrons
   (B) Protons
   (C) Neutrons
   (D) Nucleus

5. Goldstein's experiments which involved passing high voltage electricity through gases at very low pressure resulted in the discovery of __________.
   (A) Nucleus   (B) Electron
   (C) Proton   (D) Neutron

6. In which year neutron was discovered?
   (A) 1886   (B) 1897
   (C) 1932   (D) 1909

7. Which of the following is the correct electronic configuration of sodium?
   (A) 1, 2, 8   (B) 8, 2, 1
   (C) 2, 1, 8   (D) 2, 8, 1

8. The particle not present in an ordinary hydrogen atom is __________.
   (A) Electron   (B) Proton
   (C) Neutron   (D) Neils Bohr

9. The number of electrons in the atom of an element X is 15 and the number of neutron is 16. Which of the following is the correct representation of an atom of this element?
   (A) $_{16}^{15}X$ (B) $_{15}^{16}X$
   (C) $_{15}^{31}X$ (D) $_{16}^{31}X$

10. The e/m for the proton is found to be
________.

(A) 6.54×10^3 (B) 9.58×10^4

(C) 8.8×10^3 (D) 5.89×10^4

11. The mass number of two atoms X and Y is the same (40 each) but their atomic number are different (being 20 an 18, respectively). X and Y are examples of ________.

(A) Isotopes

(B) Isobars

(C) Solid and liquid

(D) Chemically similar atoms

12. The atomic number of an element X is 8 and that of element Y is 4. Both these elements can exhibit a valency of ________.

(A) 1   (B) 2

(C) 3   (D) 4

13. The number of valence electrons in a sulphide ion, S^{2-} is ________.

(A) 8   (B) 9

(C) 10   (D) 16

14. For an element Z = 9. The valency of this element will be ________.

(A) 1   (B) 2

(C) 3   (D) 4

15. Drawback of Rutherford model of atom was ________.

(A) Neutron was not known

(B) No explanation for the neutral nature of atom

(C) No explanation of isotopes

(D) Could not explain the stability of atoms

16. The four atomic species can be represented as follows. Out of these, the two species which can be termed isobars are?

(i) $^{201}_{60}X$ (ii) $^{200}_{60}X$

(iii) $^{200}_{58}X$ (iv) $^{203}_{60}X$

(A) (i) and (ii)   (B) (ii) and (iii)

(C) (iii) and (iv)   (D) (i) and (iv)

17. The atomic numbers of four elements A, B, C, and D are 12, 13, 15 and 3, respectively. The element which cannot form a cation is ________.

(A) D   (B) C

(C) B   (D) A

18. Elements having valency one are ________.

(A) Always metals

(B) Always non-metals

(C) Always metalloids

(D) Either metals or non-metals

19. The maximum number of electrons that can be accommodated in N shell of an atom is ________.

(A) 2   (B) 8

(C) 18   (D) 32

20. Isotopes of cobalt is used for treatment of which one of the following?

(A) TB

(B) Cancer

(C) Goiter

(D) Diabetes

21. The number of neutron in an atom having atomic number 11 and mass number 23 is ________.

(A) 10   (B) 11

(C) 12   (D) 13

22. The ion an element has 3 positive charges. The mass number of atom of this element is 27 and the number of neutrons is 14. What is the number of electrons in the ion?

(A) 10   (B) 13

(C) 16   (D) 14

23. The correct electronic configuration of chloride ion is ________.

(A) 2, 8   (B) 2, 8, 4

(C) 2, 8, 8   (D) 2, 8, 7

24. Which of the following represents the correct electron distribution in magnesium ion?

(A) 2, 8

(B) 2,8, 1

(C) 2, 8, 2

(D) 2, 8, 3

25. The isotopes of an element contain __________.

(A) Same number of neutrons but different number of protons

(B) Different number of neutrons but some number of protons

(C) Same number of neutrons but different number of electrons

(D) Different number of protons as well as different number of neutrons

26. Almost the entire mass of an atom is concentrated in the __________.

(A) Proton

(B) Electron

(C) Neutron

(D) Nucleus

27. The K, L and M shells of an atom are full, its atomic number is __________.

(A) 10   (B) 12

(C) 18   (D) 20

28. Which of the air pressure is appropriate for the production of cathode rays in the discharge tube?

(A) 1 mm Hg

(B) 0.001 mm Hg

(C) 1 cm Hg

(D) 0.001 cm Hg

29. The other name of $_1^1H$ is __________.

(A) Protium

(B) Deuterium

(C) Tritium

(D) Proton

30. The fixed circular paths around the nucleus are called __________.

(A) Orbitals

(B) Orbits

(C) Mesons

(D) Nucleous

HOTS (ACHIEVERS SECTION)

31. $_7N^{15}$ and $_8O^{16}$ are pair of ______

(A) Isotopes

(B) Isobars

(C) Isotones

(D) None of these

32. Which of the following statement about the electron is incorrect?

(A) It is a negatively charged particles

(B) The mass of the electron is equal to the mass of the neutron

(C) It is a basic constituent of all atom

(D) It is a constituent of cathode rays

33. In an alpha scattering experiment, few alpha particles rebounded because

(A) Most of the space in the atom is occupied

(B) Positive charge of the atoms very little space

(C) The mass of the atom is concentrated in the centre

(D) All the positive charge and mass of the atom is concentrated in small volume

34. Which of the following statements is incorrect about the structure of an atom?

  i. The whole mass of an atom is concentrated in the nucleus

 ii. The atom is an indivisible particle

iii. The atom as a whole is neutral

iv. All the atoms are stable in their basic state

Choose the right option among the following:

(A) and (iii)   (B) only (ii)

(C) (ii) and (iv)   (D) none of these

35. Which of the following is an incorrect statement in reference with observation in Rutherford's α-particle scattering experiment?

(A) Some of the α-particles rebound after hitting the gold foil

(B) Some of the particles deflected from their path

(C) Some of the particles not pass through the gold foil

(D) Most of the particles pass straight through the gold foil

CELL–THE FUNDAMENTAL UNIT OF LIFE

MULTIPLE CHOICE QUESTIONS

1. The term 'cell' was given by __________.
   (A) Robert Brown
   (B) Flemming
   (C) Robert Hooke
   (D) Leeuwen hoek

2. Who proposed the cell theory?
   (A) Watson and Crick
   (B) Schleiden and Schwann
   (C) Darwin and Wallace
   (D) Mendel and Morgan

3. Which one of the following is prokaryotic?
   (A) Blue green algae
   (B) Fungus
   (C) Fly
   (D) Plasmodium

4. Which of the following has an irregular or variable shape?
   (A) Amoeba
   (B) Euglena
   (C) Acetabularia
   (D) Paramecium

5. Nucleolus is a site of __________.
   (A) RNA synthesis
   (B) Enzyme synthesis
   (C) Ribosome
   (D) Protein synthesis

6. Genetic material of a eukaryotic cell is contained in __________.
   (A) Nucleus
   (B) Nucleoid
   (C) Nucleolus
   (D) Nucleoplasm

7. Which one of the following is called the power house of the cell?
   (A) Ribosomes
   (B) Plastids
   (C) Mitochondria
   (D) Vacuoles

8. A plant cell placed in hypotonic solution will __________.
   (A) Shrink
   (B) Swell
   (C) See no change
   (D) Face Exosmosis

9. Which one of the following is called the suicide bag of the cell?
   (A) Ribosomes
   (B) Lysosomes
   (C) Centrioles
   (D) Mitochondria

10. The longest cell in the human body is __________.
    (A) Muscle cell
    (B) Nerve cell
    (C) Kidney cell
    (D) Liver cell

11. The idea 'omins cellula a cellula' which means that all living cells arise from pre-existing cells, was given by __________.
    (A) Parkinje
    (B) Schleiden
    (C) Rudolf Virchow
    (D) Robert brown

12. Middle lamella is formed of ___________.
    (A) Calcium pectate
    (B) Cellulose
    (C) Lignin
    (D) Hemicelluloses
13. A cell placed in hypotonic solution bursts up: It is ___________.
    (A) Plant cell   (B) Fungal cell
    (C) Bacterial cell   (D) Animal cell
14. Which material is present in bulk in plasma membrane say 75%?
    (A) Phospholipids
    (B) Polysaccharides
    (C) Cholesterol
    (D) Protein
15. Bulk transport occurs through ___________.
    (A) Exoctosis
    (B) Endocytosis
    (C) Endo osmosis
    (D) Both (A) and (B)
16. Cytoplasm is ___________.
    (A) Unit mass of protoplasm
    (B) Protoplasm excluding plasma membrane
    (C) Protoplasm excluding plasma membrane and cell organelles
    (D) Protoplasm excluding plasma membrane and nucleus
17. Protein storing plastid is ___________.
    (A) Aleuroplast
    (B) Elaioplast
    (C) Omyloplast
    (D) Both (B) and (C)
18. Site of photosynthesis is ___________.
    (A) Chromoplast   (B) Leucoplast
    (C) Chloroplast   (D) Omyloplast
19. Rough ER contains ___________.
    (A) Detoxification centres
    (B) Ribosomes
    (C) Lysosomes
    (D) Carbohydrate synthesizing machinery

20. The kitchen of a cell is ___________.
    (A) Endoplasmic reticulum
    (B) Golgi apparatus
    (C) Chloroplast
    (D) Mitochondria
21. The undefined nuclear region of prokaryotes is also known as ___________.
    (A) Nucleus   (B) Nucleoid
    (C) Nucleolus   (D) Nucleic acid
22. Lysosomes arise from ___________.
    (A) Nucleus
    (B) Mitochondria
    (C) Golgi apparatus
    (D) Endoplasmic reticulum
23. The only cell organelle seen in prokaryotic cell is ___________.
    (A) Mitochondria
    (B) Plastids
    (C) Ribosomes
    (D) Lysosomes
24. Chromosomes are made up of ___________.
    (A) RNA
    (B) DNA
    (C) Protein
    (D) Both (B) and (C)
25. Find out the false statement.
    (A) Golgi apparatus is involved with the formation of lysosomes
    (B) Mitochondria is said to be the power house of the cell as ATP is generated in them
    (C) Cytoplasm is called as protoplasm
    (D) Nucleus, mitochondria and plastid have DNA, hence they are able to make their own structural proteins
26. Cell wall of which one of these is not made up cellulose?
    (A) Mango tree
    (B) Hydrilla
    (C) Bacteria
    (D) Cactus

27. Which one of the following is absent in plant cell?
(A) Mitochondria   (B) Centrioles
(C) Ribosomes   (D) Nucleus

28. Organelle without a cell membrane is __________.
(A) Chloroplast   (B) Nucleus
(C) Ribosome   (D) Mitochondrion

29. Which of the following is incorrect pair?
(A) Lysosome – Secretory granules
(B) Mitochondria – Power house of the cell
(C) Chloroplast – Kitchen of the cell
(D) Nucleus – Brain of the cell

30. The proteins and lipids, essential for building the cell membrane, are manufactured by __________.
(A) Peroxisomes
(B) Mitochondria
(C) Golgi apparatus
(D) Endoplasmic reticulum

HOTS (ACHIEVERS SECTION)

31. Which of the following structures is usually present only in animal cells?
(A) Cell wall   (B) Centrioles
(C) Nucleus   (D) Vacuoles

32. Ribosomes are made of how many sub-units?
(A) 0   (B) 2
(C) 3   (D) 4

33. Haploid cells in angiosperms can be obtained by culturing __________.
(A) young leaves   (B) Root tips
(C) endosperms   (D) pollen grains

34. Human cheek cells stained in methylene blue and mounted in glycerine were observed with the help of a compound microscope. The components of the cell which were seen are:
(A) cell wall, cytoplasm, nucleus
(B) plasma membrane, cytoplasm, nucleus, mitochondria
(C) plasma membrane, cytoplasm, nucleus
(D) plasma membrane, cytoplasm, nucleus, mitochondria, lysosomes, Golgi bodies.

35. Which of the following is not a function of the vacuole in plants?
(A) They store toxic metabolic wastes
(B) They help with the process of cell division
(C) They help to maintain turgidity
(D) They provide structural support

————Darken Your Choice with HB Pencil————

1.	Ⓐ Ⓑ Ⓒ Ⓓ	8.	Ⓐ Ⓑ Ⓒ Ⓓ	15.	Ⓐ Ⓑ Ⓒ Ⓓ	22	Ⓐ Ⓑ Ⓒ Ⓓ	29.	Ⓐ Ⓑ Ⓒ Ⓓ
2.	Ⓐ Ⓑ Ⓒ Ⓓ	9.	Ⓐ Ⓑ Ⓒ Ⓓ	16.	Ⓐ Ⓑ Ⓒ Ⓓ	23.	Ⓐ Ⓑ Ⓒ Ⓓ	30.	Ⓐ Ⓑ Ⓒ Ⓓ
3.	Ⓐ Ⓑ Ⓒ Ⓓ	10.	Ⓐ Ⓑ Ⓒ Ⓓ	17.	Ⓐ Ⓑ Ⓒ Ⓓ	24.	Ⓐ Ⓑ Ⓒ Ⓓ	31.	Ⓐ Ⓑ Ⓒ Ⓓ
4.	Ⓐ Ⓑ Ⓒ Ⓓ	11.	Ⓐ Ⓑ Ⓒ Ⓓ	18.	Ⓐ Ⓑ Ⓒ Ⓓ	25.	Ⓐ Ⓑ Ⓒ Ⓓ	32.	Ⓐ Ⓑ Ⓒ Ⓓ
5.	Ⓐ Ⓑ Ⓒ Ⓓ	12.	Ⓐ Ⓑ Ⓒ Ⓓ	19.	Ⓐ Ⓑ Ⓒ Ⓓ	26.	Ⓐ Ⓑ Ⓒ Ⓓ	33.	Ⓐ Ⓑ Ⓒ Ⓓ
6.	Ⓐ Ⓑ Ⓒ Ⓓ	13.	Ⓐ Ⓑ Ⓒ Ⓓ	20.	Ⓐ Ⓑ Ⓒ Ⓓ	27.	Ⓐ Ⓑ Ⓒ Ⓓ	34.	Ⓐ Ⓑ Ⓒ Ⓓ
7.	Ⓐ Ⓑ Ⓒ Ⓓ	14.	Ⓐ Ⓑ Ⓒ Ⓓ	21.	Ⓐ Ⓑ Ⓒ Ⓓ	28.	Ⓐ Ⓑ Ⓒ Ⓓ	35.	Ⓐ Ⓑ Ⓒ Ⓓ

TISSUES

6

➤ The importance of tissue
➤ Plant and animal tissues
➤ Different plant tissues
➤ The protective tissues
➤ Different animal tissues

MULTIPLE CHOICE QUESTIONS

1. Presence of tissues in a multicellular organisms ensures _______.
   (A) Body strength
   (B) Division of labour
   (C) Higher reproductive potential
   (D) Faster development

2. A group of cells alike in form, function and origin are called _______.
   (A) Organ
   (B) Organelle
   (C) Tissue
   (D) None of these

3. Parenchyma : simple :: Phloem: _______
   (A) Simple
   (B) Complex
   (C) Xylem
   (D) Collenchyma

4. Which are the four types of animal tissue?
   (A) Epithelial, connective, muscular, cardiac
   (B) Epithelial, squamous, muscular, connective
   (C) Connective, muscular, epithilial, nervous
   (D) Cuboidal, ciliated, glandular, columnar

5. The nuclei of meristematic cells are _______.
   (A) Small
   (B) Large
   (C) Medium
   (D) None of these

6. The cell wall of meristematic cell is made of _______.
   (A) Protein
   (B) Peptidoglycan
   (C) Cellulose
   (D) Aminoacid

7. _______ tissue forms new cells in plants.
   (A) Simple
   (B) Permanent
   (C) Meristematic
   (D) None of these

8. Parenchyma which contains chlorophyll is called _______.
   (A) Chlorenchyma
   (B) Collenchyma
   (C) Selerenchyma
   (D) None of these

9. Tissue that is absent in monocots is _______.
   (A) Collencyma
   (B) Aerenchyma
   (C) Sclerenchyma
   (D) Chlorenchyma

10. Grit of pear is formed of _______.
    (A) Tracheids
    (B) Companion cells
    (C) Sclereids
    (D) Sclerenchyma fibres

11. Transpiration of exchange of gases are functions of _______.

(A) Xylem
(B) Stomata
(C) Both (A) and (B)
(D) Neither (A) nor (B)

12. Cuboidal : epithelial : : Cardiac _______
(A) Epithelial   (B) Nervous
(C) Muscular   (D) Connective

13. Tendons and ligaments are _______.
(A) Loose connective tissue
(B) Dense connective tissue
(C) Muscular tissue
(D) Vascular tissue

14. Most aboundant animal tissue is _______.
(A) Blood   (B) Epithelium
(C) Muscular   (D) Connective

15. Striated muscle is also called _______.
(A) Smooth muscle
(B) Cardiac muscle
(C) Skeletal muscle
(D) Involuntary muscle

16. Which of the following components of xylem is living?
(A) Vessels
(B) Tracheids
(C) Xylem parenchyma
(D) Xylem sclerenchyma

17. Collenchyma mainly forms _______.
(A) Epidermis   (B) Hypodermis
(C) Phloem   (D) Inner cortex

18. The term tissue was given by _______.
(A) Bichat   (B) Mayer
(C) Robert Hooke   (D) Leeuwenhoek

19. A cell body which contains a nucleus and cytoplasm is _______.
(A) Tendon   (B) Ligament
(C) Neuron   (D) Blood

20. Largest blood cells are _______.
(A) Monocytes
(B) Basophils
(C) Neutrophils
(D) Lymphocytes

21. Ligament connects a bone with _______.
(A) Muscle
(B) Bone
(C) Skin
(D) Both (A) and (B)

22. Tendon connects _______.
(A) A bone with another bone
(B) A muscle with a muscle
(C) A muscle with a bone
(D) A nerve with a muscle

23. Plant length is increased by _______.
(A) Periblem
(B) Apical meristems
(C) Lateral meristems
(D) Parenchyma

24. Which of the following tissues is composed of mainly dead cells?
(A) Xylem   (B) Phloem
(C) Epidermis   (D) Endodermis

25. The cell division is restricted to _______.
(A) Secretory cells
(B) Permanent cells
(C) Meristematic cells
(D) All of these

26. Xylem is made of _______.
(A) Tracheids   (B) Vessels
(C) Both of these (D) None of these

27. Active division takes place in the cells of _______.
(A) Xylem   (B) Phloem
(C) Cambium   (D) Sclerenchyma

28. _______ tissue prevent loss of water in plants.
(A) Protective   (B) Xylem
(C) Phloem   (D) All of these

29. Ciliated epithelium is found in _______.
(A) Trachea   (B) Uterus
(C) Tongue   (D) Oesophagus

30. Which type of tissue forms glands?
(A) Epithelial   (B) Nervous
(C) Muscle   (D) Connective

31. Which type of epithelial tissue lines the inner surface of the trachea?
    (A) Columnar
    (B) Squamous
    (C) Cuboidal
    (D) Hyaline cartilage

32. Collenchyma differs from sclerenchyma in ___________.
    (A) having suberin cell walls and protoplasm.
    (B) having pectin cell walls and protoplasm.
    (C) having lignin cell walls and protoplasm.
    (D) having no protoplasm or pectin cell walls.

33. The cells that cannot be cultured as they have lost their centrioles are ___________.
    (A) chondrocytes   (B) osteocytes
    (C) neurons   (D) mast cells

34. Nissl's granules are present in ___________.
    (A) mast cells
    (B) bone cells
    (C) cartilage cells
    (D) nerve cells

35. Which of the following is the correct sequence of transportation of food in plants?
    (A) Mesophyll cells → Tracheids → Vessels → Plant parts
    (B) Mesophyll cells → Xylem vessels → Sieve tubes → Plant parts
    (C) Epidermal cells → Mesophyll cells → Sieve tube → Plant parts
    (D) Mesophyll cells → Sieve tubes → Plant parts

—Darken Your Choice with HB Pencil—

1. Ⓐ Ⓑ Ⓒ Ⓓ	8. Ⓐ Ⓑ Ⓒ Ⓓ	15. Ⓐ Ⓑ Ⓒ Ⓓ	22 Ⓐ Ⓑ Ⓒ Ⓓ	29. Ⓐ Ⓑ Ⓒ Ⓓ
2. Ⓐ Ⓑ Ⓒ Ⓓ	9. Ⓐ Ⓑ Ⓒ Ⓓ	16. Ⓐ Ⓑ Ⓒ Ⓓ	23. Ⓐ Ⓑ Ⓒ Ⓓ	30. Ⓐ Ⓑ Ⓒ Ⓓ
3. Ⓐ Ⓑ Ⓒ Ⓓ	10. Ⓐ Ⓑ Ⓒ Ⓓ	17. Ⓐ Ⓑ Ⓒ Ⓓ	24. Ⓐ Ⓑ Ⓒ Ⓓ	31. Ⓐ Ⓑ Ⓒ Ⓓ
4. Ⓐ Ⓑ Ⓒ Ⓓ	11. Ⓐ Ⓑ Ⓒ Ⓓ	18. Ⓐ Ⓑ Ⓒ Ⓓ	25. Ⓐ Ⓑ Ⓒ Ⓓ	32. Ⓐ Ⓑ Ⓒ Ⓓ
5. Ⓐ Ⓑ Ⓒ Ⓓ	12. Ⓐ Ⓑ Ⓒ Ⓓ	19. Ⓐ Ⓑ Ⓒ Ⓓ	26. Ⓐ Ⓑ Ⓒ Ⓓ	33. Ⓐ Ⓑ Ⓒ Ⓓ
6. Ⓐ Ⓑ Ⓒ Ⓓ	13. Ⓐ Ⓑ Ⓒ Ⓓ	20. Ⓐ Ⓑ Ⓒ Ⓓ	27. Ⓐ Ⓑ Ⓒ Ⓓ	34. Ⓐ Ⓑ Ⓒ Ⓓ
7. Ⓐ Ⓑ Ⓒ Ⓓ	14. Ⓐ Ⓑ Ⓒ Ⓓ	21. Ⓐ Ⓑ Ⓒ Ⓓ	28. Ⓐ Ⓑ Ⓒ Ⓓ	35. Ⓐ Ⓑ Ⓒ Ⓓ

LEARNING OBJECTIVES

- ➤ The importance of diversity
- ➤ Classification of different organisms
- ➤ The importance of evolution
- ➤ Classification of five kingdom
- ➤ Binomial nomenclature

MULTIPLE CHOICE QUESTIONS

1. Which taxonomic term may be substituted for any rank in the classification?
   (A) Class
   (B) Taxon
   (C) Genus
   (D) Species

2. Algae belong to __________.
   (A) Thallophytes
   (B) Bryophytes
   (C) Pteridophyte
   (D) All of these

3. The most primitive and simple plants whose body cannot be differentiated into stem, roots and leaves are called __________.
   (A) Bacteria
   (B) Fungus
   (C) Mushroom
   (D) Algae

4. Who is known as the father of taxonomy?
   (A) Walter G. Rosen
   (B) Ernst Mayer
   (C) Linnaeus
   (D) Charles Darwin

5. What is scientific name of wheat?
   (A) Salanum tuberosum
   (B) Triticum aestirnum
   (C) Mangi ferra
   (D) Felis catus

6. Who gave the five kingdom of classification?
   (A) Walter G. Rosen
   (B) Linnaeus
   (C) Whittaker
   (D) Charles Darwin

7. Who has divided Prokaryota (Monera) into Archea and Eubactria?
   (A) Woese
   (B) Copeland
   (C) Whittaker
   (D) Haeckel

8. Hotspots of biodiversity means __________.
   (A) Area of the Earth that contain many endemic species
   (B) Species diversity at particular areas
   (C) Species in particular niche/area
   (D) Species serves as proxy for entire communities in particular areas.

9. The science of naming organism is called __________.
   (A) Taxonomy
   (B) Classification
   (C) Nomenclature
   (D) Identification

10. The system of nomenclature evolved by Linnaeus is __________.
    (A) Mononomial
    (B) Binomial
    (C) Polynomial
    (D) Vernacular

11. The basic unit of classification is _______.
    (A) Species   (B) Genus
    (C) Variety   (D) Family

12. Genetic material of prokaryoates is called _______.
    (A) Nucleolus   (B) Mesosome
    (C) Nucleoid   (D) Plasmid

13. Amoeba belongs to kingdom _______.
    (A) Monera   (B) Protista
    (C) Fungi   (D) Animalia

14. The eukaryotic kingdom protista was created by _______.
    (A) Woese
    (B) Whittaker
    (C) Margulis and Schwartr
    (D) Heckel

15. Who proposed the concept of evolution?
    (A) Aristotle   (B) Darwin
    (C) Theophratus   (D) Linnaeus

16. The science of classification is called _______.
    (A) Biology   (B) Taxonomy
    (C) Domography   (D) None of these

17. Phylogeny is the study of _______.
    (A) Evolution of species
    (B) Development of an individual
    (C) Embryonic development of an argan
    (D) Ecological adaptation of an organisms

18. Class is a category between _______.
    (A) Family and genes
    (B) Order and family
    (C) Kingdom and phylum
    (D) Phylum and order

19. Fungi resemble animals in having _______.
    (A) Mycelium
    (B) Chitin
    (C) Glycogen
    (D) Both (B) and (C)

20. A plant body not differentiated into root, stem and leaves is termed as _______.
    (A) Herb
    (B) Thallus
    (C) Hyphae
    (D) Mycelium

21. A group of similar freely inter-breeding organisms constitutes a _______.
    (A) Class
    (B) Family
    (C) Species
    (D) Genera

22. Chlorophyll containing, autotrophic thallophytes are called _______.
    (A) Lichens
    (B) Algae
    (C) Fungi
    (D) Bryophytes

23. The ability of nitrogen fixation is found in _______.
    (A) Monerans only
    (B) Protistans only
    (C) Both monerans and protisyans
    (D) Fungi only

24. A group of related genera, with still less number of similarities as compared to the genus and species, constitutes _______.
    (A) Class
    (B) Order
    (C) Family
    (D) Division

25. The algal partner of a lichen is called _______.
    (A) Phycobiont
    (B) Mycobiont
    (C) Both (A) and (B)
    (D) None of these

26. The body of _______ has chitinous cell wall and is made up of hyphae and mycelium.
    (A) Funaria   (B) Riccia
    (C) Rhizopus   (D) Spirogyra

27. Naked seeds are present in _________.
    (A) Lemon   (B) Mango
    (C) Mustard   (D) Pinus
28. The compound plants composed of algae and fungi are called _________.
    (A) Algae   (B) Lichens
    (C) Bryophytes   (D) Pteridophytes
29. Which of the following group of plants is called vascular cryptogams?
    (A) Angiospermae
    (B) Bryophyta
    (C) Pteridophyta
    (D) Thallophyta
30. Homo : generic name :: sapiens : _______
    (A) Species name
    (B) Organism name
    (C) Human name
    (D) Division name

HOTS (ACHIEVERS SECTION)

31. Symbiosis between fungi and algae leads to the formation of _________.
    (A) algae   (B) lichens
    (C) fungi   (D) yeast
32. The kingdom Protista consists of _________.
    (A) multicellular organisms whose chromosomes are not enclosed in a nuclear membrane.
    (B) unicellular organisms whose chromosomes are not enclosed in a nuclear membrane.
    (C) multicellular organisms whose chromosomes are enclosed in a nuclear membrane.
    (D) unicellular organisms whose chromosomes are enclosed in a nuclear membrane.
33. Suppose you accidently find an old preserved permanent slide without a label. In order to identify it, you place the slide under microscope and observe the following features:
    (i)   Unicellular
    (ii) Well defined nucleus
    (iii) Biflagellate - one long flagellum, lying longitudinally and the other short flagellum.

    What would you identify it as? Also name the kingdom it belongs to.
    (A) Diatom ; Fungi
    (B) Trypanosoma ; Protozoa
    (C) Paramecium ; Protozoa
    (D) Euglena ; Protista
34. Match column I with column II and select the correct option from the codes given below.

Column I	Column II
(A) Thallophyta	(i) Marsilea
(B) Bryophyta	(ii) Pinus
(C) Pteridophyta	(iii) Ulothrix
(D) Gymnospermae	(iv) Ficus
(E) Angiospermae	(v) Funaria

    (A) (A)-(iii), (B)-(ii), (C)-(i), (D)-(iv), (E)-(v)
    (B) (A)-(i), (B)-(ii), (C)-(iii), (D)-(iv), (E)-(v)
    (C) (A)-(i), (B)-(v), (C)-(iii), (D)-(ii), (E)-(iv)
    (D) (A)-(iii), (B)-(v), (C)-(i), (D)-(ii), (E)-(iv)

35. Match column I with column II and select the correct option from the given codes.

Column I	Column II
(A) Pore bearing animals	(i) Arthropoda
(B) Cnidoblasts	(ii) Coelenterata
(C) Metameric segmentation	(iii) Porifera
(D) Jointed legs	(iv) Echinodermata
(E) Soft bodied animals	(v) Mollusca
(F) Spiny skinned animal	(vi) Annelida

(A) (A)-(iv), (B)-(v), (C)-(i), (D)-(vi), (E)-(iii), (F)-(ii)

(B) (A)-(vi), (B)-(i), (C)-(iv), (D)-(ii), (E)-(v), (F)-(iii)

(C) (A)-(iii), (B)-(ii), (C)-(vi), (D)-(i), (E)-(v), (F)-(iv)

(D) (A)-(i), (B)-(ii), (C)-(iv), (D)-(vi), (E)-(v), (F)-(iii)

1.	A B C D	8.	A B C D	15.	A B C D	22	A B C D	29.	A B C D
2.	A B C D	9.	A B C D	16.	A B C D	23.	A B C D	30.	A B C D
3.	A B C D	10.	A B C D	17.	A B C D	24.	A B C D	31.	A B C D
4.	A B C D	11.	A B C D	18.	A B C D	25.	A B C D	32.	A B C D
5.	A B C D	12.	A B C D	19.	A B C D	26.	A B C D	33.	A B C D
6.	A B C D	13.	A B C D	20.	A B C D	27.	A B C D	34.	A B C D
7.	A B C D	14.	A B C D	21.	A B C D	28.	A B C D	35.	A B C D

MOTION

LEARNING OBJECTIVES

➤ Concept of motion
➤ Different types of motion
➤ The terms – velocity, acceleration and retardation

MULTIPLE CHOICE QUESTIONS

1. What remains constant in uniform circular motion?
   (A) Speed (B) Direction
   (C) Both (A) and (B) (D) None of these

2. The quantity which is measured by the area occupied under the speed-time graph is __________.
   (A) Velocity
   (B) Distance travelled
   (C) Time taken
   (D) None of these

3. If a body moves 6 m towards South and then turns towards East and moves 8 m, the displacement of the body is __________.

   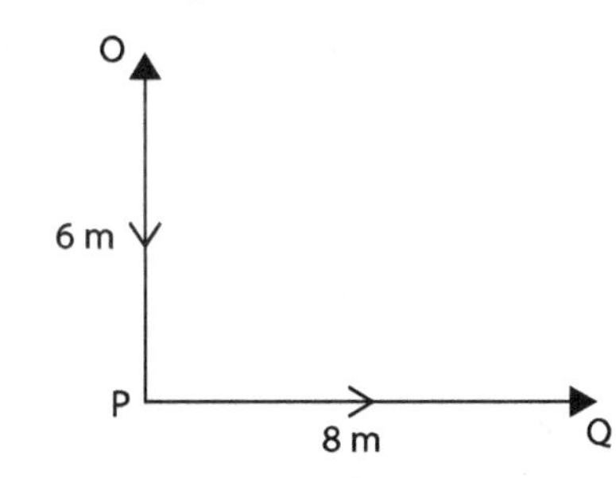

   (A) 12 m (B) 8 m
   (C) 10 m (D) 6 m

4. A man travels a distance of 2 m towards East, 6 m towards South and finally 6 m towards East. The resultant displacement is __________.
   (A) 10 m (B) 8 m
   (C) 12 m (D) 14 m

5. The motion in which a body has a constant speed but not constant velocity is called __________.
   (A) Uniform linear motion
   (B) Uniform circular motion
   (C) Rotatory motion
   (D) Vibratory motion

6. What does the slope of a velocity-time graph indicate?
   (A) Speed
   (B) Distance travelled
   (C) Velocity
   (D) Acceleration

7. What can you say about the motion of body if its speed-time graph is a straight line parallel to the time axis?
   (A) Speed of the body is zero
   (B) Speed of the body is increasing at a constant rate
   (C) Speed of the body is uniform i.e., constant
   (D) None of these

8. A car travels first 40 km at the speed of 55 km/h and next 20 km at the speed of 50 km/h. Find the total time taken by the car to reach its destination ________.
   (A) 1.34 hours   (B) 1.2 hours
   (C) 1.72 hours   (D) 1.127 hours

9. What can you say about the motion of a body whose distance–time graph is a straight line parallel to time axis?
   (A) Body is moving at same speed
   (B) Body is at rest
   (C) Both body and time are at rest
   (D) None of these

10. What conclusion can you draw about the acceleration of a body from the speed–time graph shown below?

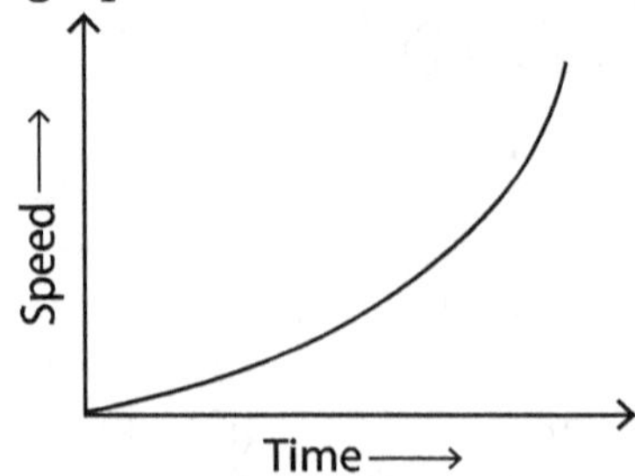

   (A) Positive acceleration
   (B) Deceleration
   (C) Non-uniform acceleration
   (D) Uniform acceleration

11. It is possible for an object to accelerate but not to change its speed if it moves ________.

   (A) In a circular track
   (B) On a sloppy hill
   (C) On a straight path
   (D) To and fro

12. Find the acceleration of a cyclist whose speed changes from 30 m/s to 45 m/s in 3 seconds.
    (A) 3 m/s²   (B) –3 m/s²
    (C) 5 m/s²   (D) –5 m/s²

13. Which of these, decides the direction of motion of the body?
    (A) Speed   (B) Velocity
    (C) Distance   (D) Acceleration

14. The figure shows distance–time graphs of two cars A and B running at different speeds. Which car is running with a greater speed in comparison to the other car?

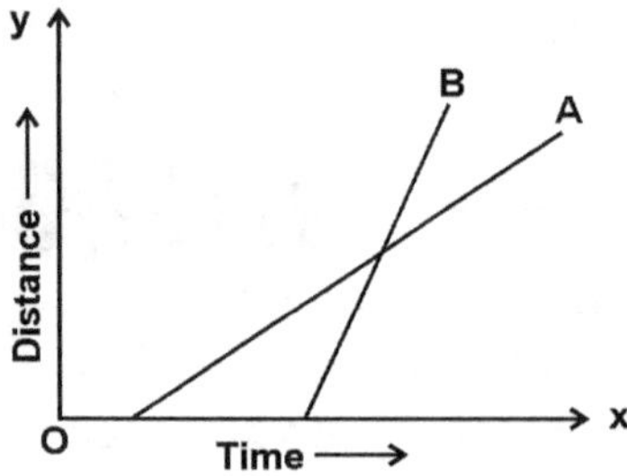

    (A) Car A is running faster than B
    (B) Car B is running faster than A
    (C) Both A and B have same speed
    (D) None of these

15. A bus increases its speed from 36 km/h to 72 km/h in 10 seconds. Its acceleration is ________.
    (A) 5 m/s²   (B) 2 m/s²
    (C) 3.6 m/s²   (D) 1 m/s²

16. A bus moving along a straight line at 15 m/s undergoes an acceleration 2.5 m/s². After 2 seconds, its speed will be ________.
    (A) 20 m/s   (B) 26 m/s
    (C) 25 m/s   (D) 30 m/s

17. The area under a speed–time graph represents a physical quantity which has the unit ________.
    (A) m   (B) ms
    (C) ms⁻¹   (D) ms⁻²

18. If the displacement of an object is proportional to the square of time, then the object is moving with

OLYMPIAD WORKBOOK (NSO) CLASS– 9

(A) Uniform velocity
(B) Uniform acceleration
(C) Increasing acceleration
(D) Decreasing acceleration

19. What is the distance covered by a particle during the time interval of 20 seconds, for which the speed–time graph is shown in the adjacent figure?
(A) 400 m   (B) 100 m
(C) 200 m   (D) All of these

20. Four cyclists A, B, C, and D are cycling on a levelled straight road. Their distance–time graphs are shown in the given figure. Which of the following is correct regarding the motion of these cyclists?

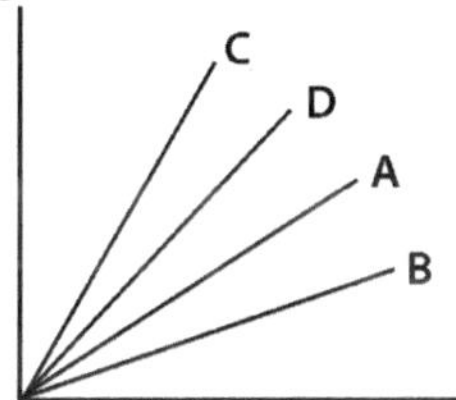

(A) Cyclist A is faster than D
(B) Cyclist B is the slowest
(C) Cyclist D is faster than C
(D) Cyclist C is the slowest

21. A car of mass 1000 kg is moving with a velocity of 10 ms^{-1}. If the velocity–time graph for this car is a horizontal line parallel to the time–axis, then the velocity of car at the end of 25 s will be _______.
(A) 10 ms^{-1} (B) 25 ms^{-1}
(C) 125 ms^{-1} (D) 40 ms^{-1}

22. An object moving with a velocity of 30 m/s decelerate at the rate of 1.5 m/s^2. Find the time taken by the object to come to rest _______.
(A) 10 seconds   (B) 20 seconds
(C) 15 seconds   (D) 30 seconds

23. A car accelerates from 15 km/h to 60 km/h in 300 seconds. Find the distance travelled by the car during this time _______.
(A) 3.35 km   (B) 3.1 km
(C) 4.33 km   (D) 5 km

24. A motor cycle is being driven at a speed of 20 m/s when a brakes are applied to bring it to rest in five seconds. The deceleration produced in this case will be _______.
(A) + 4 m/s^2 (B) –4 m/s^2
(C) +0.25 m/s^2 (D) –0.25 m/s^2

25. An artificial satellite is moving in a circular orbit of radius 32,000 km. If it takes 30 hours to complete one revolution around the earth, then find the velocity of the satellite _______.
(A) 9428 km/h   (B) 9500 km/h
(C) 6704 km/h   (D) 7295 km/h

26. A cyclist takes 3 minutes to complete one round of the circular track. If the radius of the circular track is 45 metres, then the speed of the cyclist is _______.
(A) 1.57 m/s   (B) 3.14 m/s
(C) 4.25 m/s   (D) 5.67 m/s

27. A sprinter is running along the circumference of a big stadium with a uniform speed. Which of the following is changing in this case?

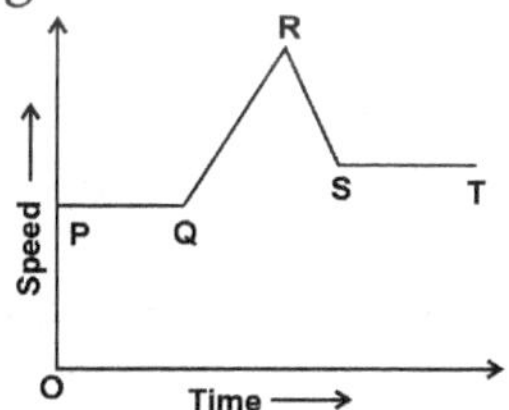

(A) Magnitude of acceleration being produced
(B) Distance covered by the sprinter per second
(C) Direction in which the sprinter is running
(D) Centripetal force acting on the sprinter

28. In the speed-time graph for a moving object shown here, the part which indicates uniform deceleration of the object is _______.
(A) ST   (B) QR
(C) RS   (D) PQ

29. Which one of the following is most likely not a case of uniform circular motion?
(A) Motion of the earth around the sun
(B) Motion of a racing car on a circular track
(C) Motion of a toy train on a circular track
(D) Motion of hours' hand on the dial of a clock

30. A train starting from rest attains a velocity of 72 km/h in 5 minutes. Assuming that the acceleration is uniform, find the distance travelled by the train for attaining this velocity.
(A) 5 km
(B) 7 km
(C) 6 km
(D) 3 km

HOTS (ACHIEVERS SECTION)

31. **Statement 1:** Displacement of a body along circular path is zero whereas its distance travelled is 2 πr.
Statement 2: The straight line distance between initial and final positions will be zero.
(A) Statement 1 is true but statement 2 is false
(B) Statement 2 is true but statement 1 is false
(C) Both statement 1 and statement 2 are true but statement 2 is not the correct reason for statement 1
(D) Both statement 1 and 2 are true and statement 2 is correct reason for statement 1.

Direction (32–35): Fill in the blanks with the correct option:

32. The motion of an object along a straight line is called ____________.
(A) Uniform motion
(B) Non-uniform motion
(C) Linear motion
(D) None of these

33. The motion of an object on a circular path is called ____________.
(A) Uniform motion
(B) Non-uniform motion
(C) Circular motion
(D) Linear motion

34. The motion of an object along its axis on fixed point is called ____________.
(A) Rotatory motion
(B) Linear motion
(C) Uniform motion
(D) None-uniform motion

35. The motion of a body travelling equal distances in equal intervals of time is called ____________.
(A) Linear motion
(B) Uniform motion
(C) Non-uniform motion
(D) Vibratory motion

—Darken Your Choice with HB Pencil—

1.	Ⓐ Ⓑ Ⓒ Ⓓ	8.	Ⓐ Ⓑ Ⓒ Ⓓ	15.	Ⓐ Ⓑ Ⓒ Ⓓ	22	Ⓐ Ⓑ Ⓒ Ⓓ	29.	Ⓐ Ⓑ Ⓒ Ⓓ
2.	Ⓐ Ⓑ Ⓒ Ⓓ	9.	Ⓐ Ⓑ Ⓒ Ⓓ	16.	Ⓐ Ⓑ Ⓒ Ⓓ	23.	Ⓐ Ⓑ Ⓒ Ⓓ	30.	Ⓐ Ⓑ Ⓒ Ⓓ
3.	Ⓐ Ⓑ Ⓒ Ⓓ	10.	Ⓐ Ⓑ Ⓒ Ⓓ	17.	Ⓐ Ⓑ Ⓒ Ⓓ	24.	Ⓐ Ⓑ Ⓒ Ⓓ	31.	Ⓐ Ⓑ Ⓒ Ⓓ
4.	Ⓐ Ⓑ Ⓒ Ⓓ	11.	Ⓐ Ⓑ Ⓒ Ⓓ	18.	Ⓐ Ⓑ Ⓒ Ⓓ	25.	Ⓐ Ⓑ Ⓒ Ⓓ	32.	Ⓐ Ⓑ Ⓒ Ⓓ
5.	Ⓐ Ⓑ Ⓒ Ⓓ	12.	Ⓐ Ⓑ Ⓒ Ⓓ	19.	Ⓐ Ⓑ Ⓒ Ⓓ	26.	Ⓐ Ⓑ Ⓒ Ⓓ	33.	Ⓐ Ⓑ Ⓒ Ⓓ
6.	Ⓐ Ⓑ Ⓒ Ⓓ	13.	Ⓐ Ⓑ Ⓒ Ⓓ	20.	Ⓐ Ⓑ Ⓒ Ⓓ	27.	Ⓐ Ⓑ Ⓒ Ⓓ	34.	Ⓐ Ⓑ Ⓒ Ⓓ
7.	Ⓐ Ⓑ Ⓒ Ⓓ	14.	Ⓐ Ⓑ Ⓒ Ⓓ	21.	Ⓐ Ⓑ Ⓒ Ⓓ	28.	Ⓐ Ⓑ Ⓒ Ⓓ	35.	Ⓐ Ⓑ Ⓒ Ⓓ

FORCE AND LAWS OF MOTION 

LEARNING OBJECTIVES

➤ Balanced and unbalanced forces
➤ Momentum and conservation of momentum
➤ Applications of the law of momentum

MULTIPLE CHOICE QUESTIONS

1. The physical quantity which makes it easier to accelerate small car than a large car is measured in the unit of _______.
   (A) m/s
   (B) kg
   (C) kg. m/s
   (D) kg. m.s^2

2. The rocket works on the principle of conservation of _______.
   (A) Mass
   (B) Energy
   (C) Velocity
   (D) Momentum

3. Assume that you were in the space in a weightless environment, will it require a force to set an object in motion?
   (A) Yes
   (B) Both (A) and (B) partly correct
   (C) No
   (D) None of these

4. A motor cycle and a car are moving on a horizontal road with the same velocity. If they are brought to rest by the application of brakes, which provide equal retardation, then _______.
   (A) Motor cycle will stop at shorter distance
   (B) Car will stop at a shorter distance
   (C) Both will stop at the same distance
   (D) Nothing can be predicted

5. Which physical quantity corresponds to the rate of change of momentum?
   (A) Energy
   (B) Acceleration
   (C) Force
   (D) Mass

6. If the mass of a body and the force acting on it are both doubled, what happens to the acceleration?
   (A) It get doubled
   (B) It is halved
   (C) It remains same
   (D) It becomes four times increased

7. The amount of force required to keep a 5 kg object moving in the right direction with a constant velocity of 2 m/s is _______.
   (A) 0 N
   (B) 0.4 N
   (C) 2 N
   (D) 10 N

8. Andy spends his holiday at rest on the sofa, watching cricket match and eating junk food. What effect does this practice have upon his inertia?
   (A) Decreases
   (B) Increases
   (C) No effect
   (D) None of these

9. A force of 5N is applied on a body of mass M to produce an acceleration of 10 ms^{-2}. The same force when applied on another body of mass 'm' produces acceleration of 20 ms^{-2}. Find the acceleration produced by the force when both the masses are combined together
   - (A) 6.6 ms^{-2}
   - (B) 2.66 ms^{-2}
   - (C) 3.66 ms^{-2}
   - (D) 4 ms^{-2}

10. A girl weighing 45 kg is standing on the floor, exerting a downward force of 200 N on the floor. The force exerted on her by the floor is _______.
   - (A) Greater than 200 N
   - (B) Less than 200 N
   - (C) Equal to 200 N
   - (D) no force exerted

11. Newton's second law of motion can be written as _______.
   - (A) Force = mass × acceleration
   - (B) Force = rate of change of momentum
   - (C) Both (A) and (B)
   - (D) neither (A) nor (B)

12. A girl of mass 20 kg having velocity 2 m/sec jumps on stationary cart of mass 2 kg. Find the velocity of the girl when the cart starts moving _______.
   - (A) 2 m/s
   - (B) 54 m/s
   - (C) 0.95 m/s
   - (D) 1.81 m/s

13. A bullet of mass 20 g is horizontally fired with a velocity of 150 m/s from a pistol of mass 2 kg. What is the recoil velocity of the pistol?
   - (A) -1.25 ms^{-1}
   - (B) -1.5 ms^{-1}
   - (C) 1.5 ms^{-1}
   - (D) 2.5 ms^{-1}

14. The property of matter due to which a body continues in its state of rest or of uniform motion unless an external force is applied on it is called _______.
   - (A) Momentum
   - (B) Elasticity
   - (C) Inertia
   - (D) Gravitational pull

15. A constant force acts on an object of mass 5 kg for a duration of 2 seconds. It increases the object's velocity from 3 m/s to 7 m/s, find the magnitude of the force applied on the object.
   - (A) 10 N
   - (B) 20 N
   - (C) 25 N
   - (D) 30 N

16. Which body would require a greater force – accelerating a body of mass 2 kg at 5 ms^{-2} or a body of mass 4 kg at 2 ms^{-2}?
   - (A) Body of mass 4 kg
   - (B) Body of mass 2 kg
   - (C) Both requires equal force
   - (D) Can't say

17. The sparks produced during sharpening of a knife against a grinding wheel leaves the rim of the wheel tangentially. This is due to _______.
   - (A) Inertia of direction
   - (B) Inertia of motion
   - (C) Inertia of rest
   - (D) Force applied

18. An object of mass 5 kg is sliding with a constant velocity of 10 m/s on a frictionless horizontal table. The force required to keep this object moving with the same velocity is _______.
   - (A) 8 N
   - (B) 4 N
   - (C) 2 N
   - (D) 0 N

19. For a stationary body _______.
   - (A) There is no force acting on it
   - (B) The body is in vacuum
   - (C) The force acting on it is not in contact with it
   - (D) The combination of forces acting on it balances each other

20. A batsman hits back a ball straight in the direction of the bowler without changing its initial speed of 12 m/s. If the mass of the ball is 0.15 kg, the impulse imported on the ball is _______.
   - (A) 4.2 Ns
   - (B) 2.8 Ns
   - (C) 3.6 kg m/sec
   - (D) 1.6 Ns

21. According to the third law of motion, action and reaction ________.
   (A) Always act on different bodies in opposite directions
   (B) Always act on the same body but in opposite directions
   (C) Have same magnitudes and direction
   (D) Act on either body at normal to each other

22. A force of 5 N gives a mass M_1, an acceleration equal to 8 ms^{-2} and m_2 an acceleration of 24 ms^{-2} What is the acceleration if both the masses are tied together?
   (A) 3 ms^{-2}
   (B) 4 ms^{-2}
   (C) 6 ms^{-2}
   (D) 12 ms^{-2}

23. A body of mass 50 kg standing on ground exerts a force of 500 N on the ground. The force exerted by the ground on the body will be ________.
   (A) 50 N
   (B) 25000 N
   (C) 10 N
   (D) 500 N

24. A sports car, a matador, a bus and a truck are all running at the same speed of 70 km/h under identical conditions. If all these car are hit from behind with the same force and they continue to move forward, the maximum acceleration will be produced in ________.
   (A) Truck
   (B) Matador
   (C) Sports car
   (D) Bus

25. A player stops a football weighing 0.5 kg which comes flying towards him with a velocity of 10 m/s. If the impact lasts for $\frac{1}{50}$th second and the ball bounces back with a velocity of 15 m/s, then the average force involved is ________.
   (A) 625 N
   (B) 525 N
   (C) 425 N
   (D) 325 N

26. The acceleration produced by a force of 5 N acting a mass of 20 kg in m/s^2 is ________.
   (A) 4
   (B) 100
   (C) 0.25
   (D) 2.5

27. For years space travel was believed to be impossible because there was nothing which rockets could push off in space in order to provide the propulsion necessary to accelerate. This inability of a rocket to provide propulsion is because ________.
   (A) Space is void of air and so there is no air resistance in space
   (B) Rockets do accelerate in space and have been able to do so for a long time
   (C) Gravity is absent in space
   (D) Space is void of air, so the rockets have nothing to push off

28. A ball of mass m is thrown vertically upwards. What is the rate at which the momentum of the ball changes?
   (A) Zero
   (B) Infinity
   (C) mg
   (D) Data is not sufficient

29. A fielder pulls his hands backward while catching the fast running cricket ball This enables the fielder to ________.
   (A) Exert a larger force on the ball by increasing time to catch
   (B) Reduce the force exerted by the ball by increasing the time to catch
   (C) Increase the rate of change of momentum
   (D) keep the ball in hands frimly.

30. Calculate the change in momentum of a body weighing 10 kg when its velocity decreases from 20 m/s to 0.2 m/s.
   (A) –198 Ns
   (B) 204 Ns
   (C) +198 Ns
   (D) –204 Ns

31. **Statement 1:** A cricket fielder moves his hands backwards on catching a fast running cricket ball to increase the momentum of ball to maximum.

    Statement 2: The rate of change of momentum of a body is directly proportional to the applied force, and takes place in the direction in which the force acts.

    (A) Statement 1 is true but statement 2 is false.
    (B) Statement 2 is true but statement 1 is false
    (C) Both statement 1 and statement 2 are true but statement 2 is not the correct reason for statement 1
    (D) Both statement 1 and statement 2 are true and statement 2 is the correct reason for statement 1.

32. The distance 'd' covered in time 't' by a body having velocity 'v_0' and having a constant acceleration 'a' is given by $d = v_0 + \dfrac{1}{2}at^2$. This result follows from ____________.

    (A) Newton's First Law
    (B) Newton's Third Law
    (C) Newton's Second Law
    (D) None of these

33. When the speed of an object is doubled, the ratio of its kinetic energy to its momentum ____________.

    (A) gets doubled
    (B) remains the same
    (C) becomes half
    (D) becomes four times

34. A force of 10 N displaces an object through 20 cm and does work of 1 J in the process. Find the angle between the force and displacement ____________.

    (A) $\theta = 60°$ (B) $\theta = 30°$
    (C) $\theta = 35°$ (D) $\theta = 45°$

35. A plot of velocity versus time is shown in figure. A single force acts on the body. The correct statement is ____________.

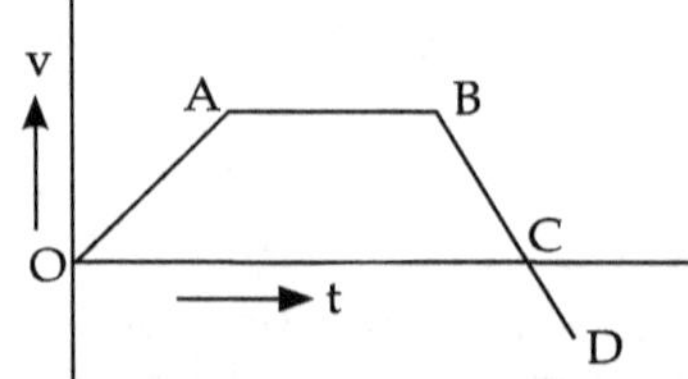

    (A) In moving from C to D, work done by the force on the body is positive.
    (B) In moving from O to A, work is done by the body and is negative.
    (C) In moving from B to C, work done by the force on the body is positive.
    (D) In moving from A to B, the body does work on the system.

————Darken Your Choice with HB Pencil————

1. Ⓐ Ⓑ Ⓒ Ⓓ	8. Ⓐ Ⓑ Ⓒ Ⓓ	15. Ⓐ Ⓑ Ⓒ Ⓓ	22 Ⓐ Ⓑ Ⓒ Ⓓ	29. Ⓐ Ⓑ Ⓒ Ⓓ
2. Ⓐ Ⓑ Ⓒ Ⓓ	9. Ⓐ Ⓑ Ⓒ Ⓓ	16. Ⓐ Ⓑ Ⓒ Ⓓ	23. Ⓐ Ⓑ Ⓒ Ⓓ	30. Ⓐ Ⓑ Ⓒ Ⓓ
3. Ⓐ Ⓑ Ⓒ Ⓓ	10. Ⓐ Ⓑ Ⓒ Ⓓ	17. Ⓐ Ⓑ Ⓒ Ⓓ	24. Ⓐ Ⓑ Ⓒ Ⓓ	31. Ⓐ Ⓑ Ⓒ Ⓓ
4. Ⓐ Ⓑ Ⓒ Ⓓ	11. Ⓐ Ⓑ Ⓒ Ⓓ	18. Ⓐ Ⓑ Ⓒ Ⓓ	25. Ⓐ Ⓑ Ⓒ Ⓓ	32. Ⓐ Ⓑ Ⓒ Ⓓ
5. Ⓐ Ⓑ Ⓒ Ⓓ	12. Ⓐ Ⓑ Ⓒ Ⓓ	19. Ⓐ Ⓑ Ⓒ Ⓓ	26. Ⓐ Ⓑ Ⓒ Ⓓ	33. Ⓐ Ⓑ Ⓒ Ⓓ
6. Ⓐ Ⓑ Ⓒ Ⓓ	13. Ⓐ Ⓑ Ⓒ Ⓓ	20. Ⓐ Ⓑ Ⓒ Ⓓ	27. Ⓐ Ⓑ Ⓒ Ⓓ	34. Ⓐ Ⓑ Ⓒ Ⓓ
7. Ⓐ Ⓑ Ⓒ Ⓓ	14. Ⓐ Ⓑ Ⓒ Ⓓ	21. Ⓐ Ⓑ Ⓒ Ⓓ	28. Ⓐ Ⓑ Ⓒ Ⓓ	35. Ⓐ Ⓑ Ⓒ Ⓓ

GRAVITATION

LEARNING OBJECTIVES

➤ The universal law of gravitation
➤ The equations of motion of freely falling body

➤ Mass and weight
➤ Kepler's laws of planetary motion
➤ The Archimedes' principle

MULTIPLE CHOICE QUESTIONS

1. A truck falls from a bridge into the river in 0.5 s. let $g = 10$ ms^{-2}, what is the height of the bridge from the surface of water?
   (A) 1 m (B) 1.25 m
   (C) 2 m (D) 2.25 m

2. SI unit of gravitational constant is ________.
   (A) Nm^2 kg^2 (B) Nm^2 kg^{-2}
   (C) Nm kg^2 (D) Nm^{2}s^{-2}

3. If the distance between two bodies is doubled, the force of attraction F between them will be ________.
   (A) 1/4 F (B) 1/2 F
   (C) 3/2 F (D) F

4. The force of gravitation between two bodies in the universe does not depend on ________.
   (A) The distance between them
   (B) Product of their masses
   (C) The total of their masses
   (D) The gravitationl constant

5. The fundamental force which holds the planets in their orbits around the sun is ______.
   (A) Gravitational pull of earth
   (B) Nuclear force of attraction
   (C) Electrostatic force of attraction
   (D) Gravitational force of attraction

6. Two objects of mass 200 kg and 800 kg are separated by a distance of 50 m. Find the gravitational force between the two bodies.
   (A) 4.26×10^{-9} N (B) 2.4×10^{-8} N
   (C) 2×10^{-9} N (D) 4.2×10^{-11} N

7. When an object is thrown up, the force of gravity ________.
   (A) Is opposite to the direction of motion
   (B) Is in the same direction as to the direction of motion
   (C) Becomes zero at the highest point
   (D) Increases as it rises up

8. A ball is dropped from a certain height. Find the speed of the ball at the end of 2 seconds.
   (A) 9.8 m/s (b 19.6 m/s
   (C) 28.4 m/s (D) 29.6m/s

9. A ball is thrown upward with the speed of 19.6 m/s, find the speed of ball after 3 seconds.
   (A) −8.8 m/s (B) 6.2 m/s
   (C) 9.8 m/s (D) −9.8 m/s

10. The mass of moon is about 0.012 times that of earth and its diameter is about 0.25 times that of earth. The value of G on the moon will be _________.
   (A) Less than that on the earth
   (B) Same as that on the earth
   (C) More than that on the earth
   (D) About one-sixth of that on the earth

11. The value of g on the surface of the moon _________.
   (A) Is the same as on the earth
   (B) Is more than that on the earth
   (C) Is less than that on the earth
   (D) Keeps changing day by day

12. What is the final velocity of a body moving against gravity when it attains the maximum height?
   (A) Zero
   (B) $\dfrac{u^2}{2g}$
   (C) $\dfrac{h}{t}$
   (D) 2gh

13. A stone is dropped from a cliff. Its speed after it has fallen 100 m is _________.
   (A) 9.8 m/s
   (B) 44.2 m/s
   (C) 19.6 m/s
   (D) 98 m/s

14. Find the value of acceleration due to gravity on the surface of the moon, given mass of the moon $= 7.4 \times 10^{22}$ kg; radius of the moon $= 1740$ km; and $G = 6.7 \times 10^{-11}$ Nm^2/kg^2.
   (A) 24 m/s^2
   (B) 1.56 m/s^2
   (C) 1.63 m/s^2
   (D) 1.84 m/s^2

15. When a ball is thrown vertically upwards, it goes through a distance of 19.6 m. Find the initial velocity of the ball.
   (A) 9.8 m/s
   (B) 19.6 m/s
   (C) 28.4 m/s
   (D) 37.2 m/s

16. If acceleration due to gravity on the earth is 10 m/s^2, then the acceleration due to gravity on moon is _________.
   (A) 1.66 m/s^2
   (B) 16.6 m/s^2
   (C) 10 m/s^2
   (D) 0.166 m/s^2

17. The second equation of motion for a freely falling body starting from rest is _________.
   (A) $h = ut + \dfrac{1}{2}gt^2$
   (B) $h = -\dfrac{1}{2}gt^2$
   (C) $h = ut - \dfrac{1}{2}gt^2$
   (D) $h = \dfrac{1}{2}gt^2$

18. The acceleration due to gravity is zero at _________.
   (A) The equator
   (B) Poles
   (C) Sea level
   (D) The centre of the earth

19. A feather and a coin released simultaneously from the same height do not reach the ground at the same time because of the _________.
   (A) Resistance of the air
   (B) Force of gravity
   (C) Force of gravitation
   (D) Difference in mass

20. The weight of an object of mass 15 kg at the centre of the earth is _________.
   (A) 147 N
   (B) 147 kg
   (C) Zero
   (D) 150 N

21. A ball is thrown up with a speed of 15 m/s. How high will it go before it begins to fall (g = 9.8 m/s^2)?
   (A) 7.5 m
   (B) 11.4 m
   (C) 22.8 m
   (D) 24 m

22. A body whose weight is 120 kg on the earth. Find its weight on the surface of moon.
   (A) 10 kg
   (B) 15 kg
   (C) 20 kg
   (D) 25 kg

23. A rectangular wooden block has length, breadth and height of 50 cm, 25 cm and 10 cm, respectively. This wooden block is kept on ground in three different ways, turn by turn. Which of the following is the correct statement about the pressure exerted by this block on the ground?
   (A) The maximum pressure is exerted when the length and breadth form the base.
   (B) The maximum pressure is exerted when the length and height form the base.
   (C) The maximum pressure is exerted when the breadth and height form the base.
   (D) None of these

24. A metal in which iron can float is ________.
   (A) Sodium   (B) Magnesium
   (C) Mercury   (D) Manganese

25. Four balls A, B, C and D displace 10 ml, 24 ml, 15 ml and 12 ml of a liquid α respectively when immersed completely. The ball which will undergo the maximum apparent loss in weight will be ________.
   (A) A   (B) B
   (C) C   (D) D

26. A solid block of density 900 kg/m³ floats in oil. The oil floats on water of density 1000 kg/m³. The density of oil in kg/m³ could be ________.
   (A) 850   (B) 1050
   (C) 950   (D) 900

27. An object weight 10 N in air, when immersed fully in a liquid it weighs only 8 N. The weight of the liquid displaced by the object will be ________.
   (A) 2 N   (B) 8 N
   (C) 10 N   (D) 12 N

28. How much would a man, whose mass is 120 kg weigh on the moon?
   (A) 98 N   (B) 196 N
   (C) 600 N   (D) 120 N

29. The relative densities of four liquids P, Q, R and S are 1.26, 1.0, 0.84 and 13.6, respectively. An object is floated in all these liquids one by one. In which liquid the object will float with its maximum volume submerged under the liquid?
   (A) P   (B) Q
   (C) R   (D) S

30. The SI unit of relative density of any substance is ________.
   (A) g/cm³   (B) kg/m³
   (C) kg/m²   (D) None of these

HOTS (ACHIEVERS SECTION)

31. Match column I with column II and choose the correct option.

Column I	Column II
(A) When a body is falling vertically downward	(i) Acceleration due to gravity is taken as negative
(B) When a body is thrown vertically upward	(ii) Initial velocity is zero
(C) When a body is dropped freely from a height	(iii) Acceleration due to gravity is taken as 5 positive

   (A) (A)-(i), (B)-(iii), (C)-(ii)
   (B) (A)-(iii), (B)-(i), (C)-(ii)
   (C) (A)-(ii), (B)-(iii), (C)-(i)
   (D) (A)-(ii), (B)-(i), (C)-(iii)

32. Two bodies 'A' and 'B' having masses 'm' and '2m' respectively are kept at a distance 'd' apart. A small particle is to

be placed so that the net gravitational force on it, due to both the bodies, is zero. Its distance from the mass A should be __________.

(A) $x = \dfrac{d}{\sqrt{6}-1}$

(B) $x = \dfrac{d}{\sqrt{3}}$

(C) $x = \dfrac{d}{1+\sqrt{2}}$

(D) $x = \dfrac{d}{1-\sqrt{2}}$

33. The height at which a body has one fourth of its weight when it is on the surface of the earth is __________.
(A) at a height 2r where r is the radius of the earth.
(B) at a height r where r is the radius of the earth.
(C) at a height $\dfrac{r}{2}$ where r is the radius of the earth.
(D) at a height $\dfrac{r}{4}$ where r is the radius of the earth.

34. Read the two statements and choose the correct option.

Statement 1: The value of acceleration due to gravity of earth does not depend upon mass of the body.

Statement 2: Acceleration due to gravity is a constant quantity.

(A) Both statements 1 and 2 are true and statement 2 is the correct explanation of statement 1.
(B) Statement 1 is true but statement 2 is false.
(C) Both statements 1 and 2 are true but statement 2 is not the correct explanation of statement 1.
(D) Both statements 1 and 2 are false.

35. Which of the following is true when a Mango falls from a Mango Tree?
(A) Only the Earth attracts the Mango.
(B) Only the Mango attracts the Earth.
(C) Both Mango and Earth attract each other
(D) Both Mango and Earth repel each other

1. Ⓐ Ⓑ Ⓒ Ⓓ	8. Ⓐ Ⓑ Ⓒ Ⓓ	15. Ⓐ Ⓑ Ⓒ Ⓓ	22 Ⓐ Ⓑ Ⓒ Ⓓ	29. Ⓐ Ⓑ Ⓒ Ⓓ
2. Ⓐ Ⓑ Ⓒ Ⓓ	9. Ⓐ Ⓑ Ⓒ Ⓓ	16. Ⓐ Ⓑ Ⓒ Ⓓ	23. Ⓐ Ⓑ Ⓒ Ⓓ	30. Ⓐ Ⓑ Ⓒ Ⓓ
3. Ⓐ Ⓑ Ⓒ Ⓓ	10. Ⓐ Ⓑ Ⓒ Ⓓ	17. Ⓐ Ⓑ Ⓒ Ⓓ	24. Ⓐ Ⓑ Ⓒ Ⓓ	31. Ⓐ Ⓑ Ⓒ Ⓓ
4. Ⓐ Ⓑ Ⓒ Ⓓ	11. Ⓐ Ⓑ Ⓒ Ⓓ	18. Ⓐ Ⓑ Ⓒ Ⓓ	25. Ⓐ Ⓑ Ⓒ Ⓓ	32. Ⓐ Ⓑ Ⓒ Ⓓ
5. Ⓐ Ⓑ Ⓒ Ⓓ	12. Ⓐ Ⓑ Ⓒ Ⓓ	19. Ⓐ Ⓑ Ⓒ Ⓓ	26. Ⓐ Ⓑ Ⓒ Ⓓ	33. Ⓐ Ⓑ Ⓒ Ⓓ
6. Ⓐ Ⓑ Ⓒ Ⓓ	13. Ⓐ Ⓑ Ⓒ Ⓓ	20. Ⓐ Ⓑ Ⓒ Ⓓ	27. Ⓐ Ⓑ Ⓒ Ⓓ	34. Ⓐ Ⓑ Ⓒ Ⓓ
7. Ⓐ Ⓑ Ⓒ Ⓓ	14. Ⓐ Ⓑ Ⓒ Ⓓ	21. Ⓐ Ⓑ Ⓒ Ⓓ	28. Ⓐ Ⓑ Ⓒ Ⓓ	35. Ⓐ Ⓑ Ⓒ Ⓓ

WORK AND ENERGY

LEARNING OBJECTIVES

➤ Different types of energy
➤ The law of conservation of energy
➤ The concept of power as a unit of energy

MULTIPLE CHOICE QUESTIONS

1. The work done in lifting a 50 kg of bag from the ground to the head, height of coolie is 200 cm, by the coolie is (assume $g = 10$ m/s^2) __________.
   (A) 500 J
   (B) 1000 J
   (C) 2000 J
   (D) 10,000 J

2. A coolie carries a load of 50 N to a distance of 100 m. The work done by him is __________.
   (A) 10 N
   (B) 0
   (C) 5000 Nm
   (D) $\dfrac{1}{2}$ J

3. A child pull a toy car by applying force of 15 N at an angel of 60°. Find the work done in pulling the toy by a distance of 20 metres.
   (A) 150 J
   (B) 120 J
   (C) 130 J
   (D) 140 J

4. The P. E. of a body at a certain height is 200 J. The K.E. possessed by it when it just touches the surface of the earth is __________.
   (A) > P.E.
   (B) < P. E.
   (C) = P.E.
   (D) can't be known

5. Find the Kinetic energy of a body of mass 2 kg moving with velocity of 0.1 metre per second.
   (A) 0.1 J
   (B) 1.0 J
   (C) 0.01 J
   (D) 10.0 J

6. An object of mass 12 kgs is at a certain height above the ground. If the P.E of the object is 480 J, find the height at which the object is with respect to the ground. Given, $g = 10$ ms^{-2}.
   (A) 12 m
   (B) 4 m
   (C) 8 m
   (D) 20 m

7. Two objects of masses 1×10^{-3} kg and 4×10^{-3} kg have equal momentum. What is the ratio of their kinetic energies?
   (A) 4 : 1
   (B) 2 : 1
   (C) 16 : 1
   (D) $\sqrt{2}$: 1

8. If the speed of an object is doubled, then its kinetic energy is __________.
   (A) Doubled
   (B) Tripled
   (C) Quadrupled
   (D) Remains same

9. A man of mass 100 kg jumps to a height of 50 cm. His potential energy at the highest point is $(g = 10 \text{ m/s}^2)$ ________.
   (A) 50 J
   (B) 500 J
   (C) 1000 J
   (D) 0

10. The type of energy possessed by a simple pendulum, when is it at the mean positions?
    (A) K.E
    (B) P.E
    (C) K.E. + P. E.
    (D) Sound energy

11. Find the energy possessed by a ball of mass 550 g rolling on the surface with a speed of 25 m/sec.
    (A) 130.896 J
    (B) 138.875 J
    (C) 171.875 J
    (D) 160.472 J

12. A batsman hits the ball of mass 250 g with his bat and the ball leaves the bat with a speed of 10 m/s. Find the work done by the bat on the ball.
    (A) 10.25 J
    (B) 12.5 J
    (C) 1.25 J
    (D) 125 J

13. An iron sphere of mass 30 kg has the same diameter as an aluminium sphere whose mass is 10.5 kg. The spheres are dropped simultaneously from a cliff. When they are 10 m from the ground, they have the same _______.
    (A) Acceleration
    (B) Momentum
    (C) Kinetic energy
    (D) Potential energy

14. A 1 kg mass has a kinetic energy of 1 joule when its speed is ________.
    (A) 0.50 m/s
    (B) 1.24 m/s
    (C) 4.4 m/s
    (D) 1.4 m/s

15. If air resistance is negligible, the sum total of potential and kinetic energies of a freely falling body ________.
    (A) Increases
    (B) Decreases
    (C) Becomes zero
    (D) Remains the same

16. Work done by a string when a stone is tied to it and whirled in a circle is ________.
    (A) Positive
    (B) Negative
    (C) Zero
    (D) None of these

17. A car is accelerated on a travelled road and acquires a velocity 4 times of its initial velocity. During this process, the potential energy of the car ________.
    (A) Does not change
    (B) Becomes twice that of the initial P.E.
    (C) Decomes four times that of the initial P.E.
    (D) Becomes 16 times that of the initial P.E.

18. A car is accelerated on a levelled road and attains a speed of 4 times its initial speed. In this process, the K.E. of the car ________.
    (A) Does not change
    (B) Becomes 4 times that of initial P.E.
    (C) Becomes 8 times that of initial P.E.
    (D) Becomes 16 times that of initial P.E.

19. In case of negative work, the angle between the force and displacement is ________.
    (A) 0°
    (B) 45°
    (C) 90°
    (D) 180°

20. Two unequal masses posses the same momentum, then the Kientic energy of the heavier mass is ________ than the Kinetic energy of the lighter mass.
    (A) More
    (B) Less
    (C) Equal
    (D) Insufficient data

21. A copper ball of mass 10 kg has the same diameter as an aluminium ball of mass 3.5 kg. Both the balls are dropped simultaneously from a tower. When they are 10 m above the ground, they have the same _________.
(A) Acceleration
(B) Momentum
(C) Potential energy
(D) Kinetic energy

22. The work done on an object does not depend on the _________.
(A) Displacement
(B) Force applied
(C) Angle between force and displacement
(D) Initial velocity of the object

23. An electric bulb of 60 w is used for 6 h per day. Calculate the 'units of energy consumed in one day by the bulb _________.
(A) 0.60 'units'   (B) 0.36 'units'
(C) 0.45 'units   (D) 0.24 'units'

24. If the speed of a motor car becomes six times, then the kinetic energy becomes _____ times.
(A) 6
(B) 12
(C) 36
(D) Remains the same

25. The momentum of a bullet of mass 20 g fired from a gun is 10 kg. m/s. The kinetic energy of this bullet in kJ will be _________.
(A) 5   (B) 1.5
(C) 2.5   (D) 25

26. In which of the following situations will the potential energy of the spring be minimum?
(A) Compressed
(B) Extended
(C) In its original shape
(D) None of these

27. Each of the following statement describes a force acting. Which of these forces is causing work to be done?
(A) The weight of a book at rest on a table
(B) The pull of a moving railway engine on its coaches
(C) The tension in an elastic band wrapped around a parcel
(D) The push of a person's feet when standing on the floor

28. When a stone is thrown upward with a certain speed, then its kinetic energy at the highest point is _________.
(A) Maximum
(B) Minimum
(C) Zero
(D) None of these

29. A girl weighing 400 N climbs a vertical ladder. If the value of g be 10 ms^{-2}, the work doen by her after climbing 2 m will be _________.
(A) 200 J
(B) 80 J
(C) 2000 J
(D) 800 J

30. Which of the following energy change involves frictional force?
(A) Chemical energy to heat energy
(B) Kinetic energy to heat energy
(C) Potential energy to sound energy
(D) Chemical energy to kinetic energy

31. The bulb glows because of electricity. Identify the energy conversion in this process.
    (A) Light energy into electrical energy
    (B) Electrical energy into light energy
    (C) Chemical energy into heat energy
    (D) Light energy into heat energy

32. A ball is released from certain height. Which of the following statement is correct about this example?
    (A) Kinetic energy decreases at each second.
    (B) Potential energy decreases at each second.
    (C) Total energy decreases at each second.
    (D) All of these

33. In which of the following examples does the work done not be zero?

    (A) The stone is rolling on frictionless surface with constant velocity.
    (B) A small child pushes a truck but truck remains stationary.
    (C) Moon revolve around earth because of gravitational force exerted by earth.
    (D) None of these

34. The stone of mass 3.5 kg is height of 165 cm. Calculate potential energy contained in that stone.
    (A) 52.6 J   (B) 54.6 J
    (C) 56.6 J   (D) 58.6 J

35. A bulb of rating 52 watt is on for 2 hours. Calculate energy consumed by the bulb.
    (A) 374.4 KJ   (B) 372.4 KJ
    (C) 370.4 KJ   (D) 368.4 KJ

—Darken Your Choice with HB Pencil—

1.	Ⓐ Ⓑ Ⓒ Ⓓ	8.	Ⓐ Ⓑ Ⓒ Ⓓ	15.	Ⓐ Ⓑ Ⓒ Ⓓ	22	Ⓐ Ⓑ Ⓒ Ⓓ	29.	Ⓐ Ⓑ Ⓒ Ⓓ
2.	Ⓐ Ⓑ Ⓒ Ⓓ	9.	Ⓐ Ⓑ Ⓒ Ⓓ	16.	Ⓐ Ⓑ Ⓒ Ⓓ	23.	Ⓐ Ⓑ Ⓒ Ⓓ	30.	Ⓐ Ⓑ Ⓒ Ⓓ
3.	Ⓐ Ⓑ Ⓒ Ⓓ	10.	Ⓐ Ⓑ Ⓒ Ⓓ	17.	Ⓐ Ⓑ Ⓒ Ⓓ	24.	Ⓐ Ⓑ Ⓒ Ⓓ	31.	Ⓐ Ⓑ Ⓒ Ⓓ
4.	Ⓐ Ⓑ Ⓒ Ⓓ	11.	Ⓐ Ⓑ Ⓒ Ⓓ	18.	Ⓐ Ⓑ Ⓒ Ⓓ	25.	Ⓐ Ⓑ Ⓒ Ⓓ	32.	Ⓐ Ⓑ Ⓒ Ⓓ
5.	Ⓐ Ⓑ Ⓒ Ⓓ	12.	Ⓐ Ⓑ Ⓒ Ⓓ	19.	Ⓐ Ⓑ Ⓒ Ⓓ	26.	Ⓐ Ⓑ Ⓒ Ⓓ	33.	Ⓐ Ⓑ Ⓒ Ⓓ
6.	Ⓐ Ⓑ Ⓒ Ⓓ	13.	Ⓐ Ⓑ Ⓒ Ⓓ	20.	Ⓐ Ⓑ Ⓒ Ⓓ	27.	Ⓐ Ⓑ Ⓒ Ⓓ	34.	Ⓐ Ⓑ Ⓒ Ⓓ
7.	Ⓐ Ⓑ Ⓒ Ⓓ	14.	Ⓐ Ⓑ Ⓒ Ⓓ	21.	Ⓐ Ⓑ Ⓒ Ⓓ	28.	Ⓐ Ⓑ Ⓒ Ⓓ	35.	Ⓐ Ⓑ Ⓒ Ⓓ

SOUND

MULTIPLE CHOICE QUESTIONS

1. When a wave travels through medium __________.
   (A) Energy is transferred in a periodic manner
   (B) Energy is transferred at a constant speed
   (C) Particles are transferred from one place to another
   (D) All statements are correct

2. Which of the following can produce longitudinal waves as well as transverse waves under different conditions?
   (A) Water
   (B) Slinky
   (C) T.V. transmitter
   (D) Tuning fork

3. Which of the following statements best describes frequency?
   (A) The distance travelled by a wave per second
   (B) The distance between one crest of a wave and the next one
   (C) The number of complete vibrations per second
   (D) The maximum disturbance caused by a wave

4. A boy fires a gun and hears the echo 2 seconds later. If he is 480 m away from a wall, what will be the velocity of sound in air?
   (A) 240 ms^{-1} (B) 480 ms^{-1}
   (C) 960 ms^{-1} (D) 120 ms^{-1}

5. If the speed of a wave is 340 m/s and its frequency is 1700 Hz, then λ for this wave in cm will be __________.
   (A) 0.2 (B) 2
   (C) 20 (D) 200

6. Which of the following vibrates when a musical note is produced by the cymbals in an orchestra?
   (A) Air coloumns
   (B) Metal plates
   (C) Stretched strings
   (D) Stretched membranes

7. A musical instrument is producing a continuous note. This note cannot be heard by a person having a normal hearing range. To hear, such notes must be passing through __________.
   (A) Wax (B) Vacuum
   (C) Water (D) Empty vessel

8. A girl claps and hears the echo after reflection from cliff which is 660 m away. If the velocity of sound is 330 m/s, the time taken for hearing the echo will be __________.

(A) 4s   (B) 3s
(C) 2s   (D) 8s

9. We can distinguish between the musical sounds produced by different singers on the basis of the characteristic of sound called?

(A) Pitch   (B) Timbre
(C) Loudness   (D) Frequency

10. What will be the frequency of a sound wave whose time period is 0.05s?

(A) 10 Hz   (B) 15 Hz
(C) 20 Hz   (D) 30 Hz

11. Which one of the following does not consist of transverse waves?

(A) TV signals from a satellite
(B) Light emitted by a CFL
(C) Ripples on the surface of a pond
(D) Musical notes of an orchestra

12. The maximum speed of vibrations which produce audible sound will be in __________.

(A) Sea water
(B) Ground glass
(C) Human blood
(D) Dry air

13. The sound waves travel faster __________.

(A) In solids   (B) In gases
(C) In vacuum   (D) In liquids

14. The frequency of a wave travelling at a speed of 500 ms^{-1} is 25 Hz. Its time period will be __________.

(A) 0.05s   (B) 0.04s
(C) 20s   (D) 25s

15. A ship on the surface of water sends a signal and receives it back after 4 seconds from a submarine inside the water. Calculate the distance of the submarine from the ship. (the speed of sound in water is 1450 ms^{-1})

(A) 2900 m   (B) 1450 m
(C) 3900 m   (D) 1950 m

16. If the sound wave produced by a vibrating tunning fork shown in the diagram, half the wavelength is represented by __________.

(A) AB   (B) DE
(C) BD   (D) AE

17. Which kind of sound is produced in an earthquake before the main shock wave begins?

(A) Infrasound
(B) Ultrasound
(C) Audible sound
(D) None of these

18. Which of the following device does not work on the multiple reflections of sound waves?

(A) Hydrophone
(B) Soundboard
(C) Megaphone
(D) Stethoscope

19. Bats detect obstacles in their path by receiving the reflected __________.

(A) Radiowaves
(B) Ultrasonic waves
(C) Radio waves
(D) Electro-magnetic waves

20. When sound travels through air, the air particles __________.

(A) Vibrate along the direction of wave propagation
(B) Vibrate perpendicular to the direction of wave propagation
(C) Vibrate but not in any fixed position
(D) Do not vibrate

21. Before playing the orchestra in a musical concert, a sitarist tries to adjust the tension and pluck the strings suitably. By doing so he is adjusting __________.
   (A) Amplitude of sound only
   (B) Intensity of sound only
   (C) Frequency of the sitar string with the frequency of other musical instruments
   (D) Loudness of sound

22. The ultrasound waves can penetrate into matter to a large extent because they have __________.
   (A) Very high frequency
   (B) Very high speed
   (C) Very high amplitude
   (D) Very high wavelength

23. An echo-sounder in a trawler (fishing boat) receives an echo from a shoal of fish 0.4 s after it was sent. If the speed of sound in water is 1500 m/s, how deep is the shoal?
   (A) 7500 m   (B) 600 m
   (C) 150 m   (D) 300 m

24. The vibrations of the pressure variations inside the inner car are converted into electrical signals by the __________.
   (A) Cochlea
   (B) Anvil
   (C) Hammer
   (D) Stirrup

25. Vibrations inside the ear are amplified by the three bones namely the _______ in the middle ear __________.
   (A) Hammer, anvil and pinna
   (B) Hammer, anvil and stirrup
   (C) Auditory bone, anvil and stirrup
   (D) Hammer, cochlea and stirrup

HOTS (ACHIEVERS SECTION)

26. **Statement 1:** The incident sound wave, the reflected sound wave and the normal at the point of incidence all lie in the same plane.

   Statement 2: The angle of reflection of sound is always equal to the angle of incidence of sound.
   (A) Statement 1 is true but statement 2 is false
   (B) Statement 1 is false but statement 2 is true
   (C) Both statement 1 and statement 2 are true but statement 2 is not the correct reason for statement 1
   (D) Both statement 1 and statement 2 are true and statement 2 is the correct reason for statement 1

Direction (27–28): See the figure and choose the correct option.

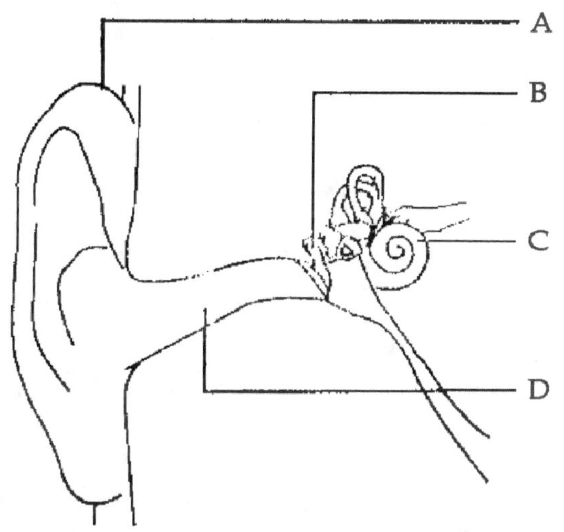

27. It collects the sound from the surrounding.
   (A) A   (B) B
   (C) C   (D) D

28. It converts the sounds into electrical signals and then send to the brain via auditory nerve.

(A) A
(B) B
(C) C
(D) D

Directions (29–30): Fill in the blanks with appropriate option.

29. Sound waves do not travel through __________

(A) Solids
(B) Liquids
(C) Gases
(D) Vacuum

30. The frequency which is not audible to the human ear is __________

(A) 5000 Hz
(B) 50000 Hz
(C) 500 Hz
(D) 50 Hz

1.	Ⓐ Ⓑ Ⓒ Ⓓ	7.	Ⓐ Ⓑ Ⓒ Ⓓ	13.	Ⓐ Ⓑ Ⓒ Ⓓ	19	Ⓐ Ⓑ Ⓒ Ⓓ	25.	Ⓐ Ⓑ Ⓒ Ⓓ
2.	Ⓐ Ⓑ Ⓒ Ⓓ	8.	Ⓐ Ⓑ Ⓒ Ⓓ	14.	Ⓐ Ⓑ Ⓒ Ⓓ	20.	Ⓐ Ⓑ Ⓒ Ⓓ	26.	Ⓐ Ⓑ Ⓒ Ⓓ
3.	Ⓐ Ⓑ Ⓒ Ⓓ	9.	Ⓐ Ⓑ Ⓒ Ⓓ	15.	Ⓐ Ⓑ Ⓒ Ⓓ	21.	Ⓐ Ⓑ Ⓒ Ⓓ	27.	Ⓐ Ⓑ Ⓒ Ⓓ
4.	Ⓐ Ⓑ Ⓒ Ⓓ	10.	Ⓐ Ⓑ Ⓒ Ⓓ	16.	Ⓐ Ⓑ Ⓒ Ⓓ	22.	Ⓐ Ⓑ Ⓒ Ⓓ	28.	Ⓐ Ⓑ Ⓒ Ⓓ
5.	Ⓐ Ⓑ Ⓒ Ⓓ	11.	Ⓐ Ⓑ Ⓒ Ⓓ	17.	Ⓐ Ⓑ Ⓒ Ⓓ	23.	Ⓐ Ⓑ Ⓒ Ⓓ	29.	Ⓐ Ⓑ Ⓒ Ⓓ
6.	Ⓐ Ⓑ Ⓒ Ⓓ	12.	Ⓐ Ⓑ Ⓒ Ⓓ	18.	Ⓐ Ⓑ Ⓒ Ⓓ	24.	Ⓐ Ⓑ Ⓒ Ⓓ	30.	Ⓐ Ⓑ Ⓒ Ⓓ

WHY DO WE FALL ILL

LEARNING OBJECTIVES

➤ The factors affecting health
➤ Disease-causing factors
➤ Infectious and non-infectious diseases

MULTIPLE CHOICE QUESTIONS

1. Infectious diseases spread through ________.
   (A) Water
   (B) Sexual
   (C) Vectors
   (D) All of these

2. Common cold is ________.
   (A) A genetic disorder
   (B) An acute disease
   (C) A chronic disease
   (D) A congenital disease

3. Pain in abdomen is ________.
   (A) Symptom
   (B) Effect
   (C) Sign
   (D) Cause

4. Which one of diseases is not infectious?
   (A) Leprosy
   (B) Leukemia
   (C) Measles
   (D) Typhoid

5. Which of the following is non-communicable disease?
   (A) Malaria
   (B) Diarrhoea
   (C) Allergy
   (D) Tuberculosis

6. A protozoan disease is ________.
   (A) Kala-azar
   (B) Malaria
   (C) Sleeping sickness
   (D) All of these

7. Which one of the following is the intrinsic factor of disease?
   (A) Tobacco
   (B) Alcohol
   (C) Environment
   (D) Hormonal imbalance

8. The insect vectors which cause yellow fever is ________.
   (A) Aedes
   (B) Culex
   (C) Anopheles mosquitoes
   (D) House fly

9. What is other name of rabies?
   (A) Ophidiophobia
   (B) Hydrophobia
   (C) Herpetophobia
   (D) Chemophobia

10. A communicable disease is caused by ________.
    (A) Allergy
    (B) Pathogen
    (C) Hormonal balance
    (D) Metabolic disorder

11. Ascariasis spreads through ________.

(A) Formites
(B) Droplets
(C) Contaminated food and water
(D) Vectors

12. The anti-viral proteins are known as __________.

(A) Antibodies   (B) Interferons
(C) Antibiotics   (D) Virus protein

13. Acne are caused by __________.
(A) Staphylococcus
(B) Leishmania
(C) Trypanosoma
(D) H_1N_1 virus

14. A disease transmitted through sexual contact is __________.
(A) HIV   (B) Syphylis
(C) Gonorrhoea   (D) All of these

15. Clean drinking water is related to __________.

(A) Public hygiene
(B) Personal hygiene
(C) Social status
(D) Economic status

16. Match the diseases with their agent.

S. No.	Disease		Agents
i.	T.B.	A.	Vibro cholerae
ii.	Ring worm	B.	Wuchereria Histalytica
iii.	Cholera	C.	Fungi
iv.	Elephantitis	D.	Mycobacterium Tuberculosis

(A) i - A, ii - C, iii - A, iv - D
(B) i - D, ii - B, iii - A, iv - C
(C) i - D, ii - C, iii - A, iv - B
(D) i - C, ii - D, iii - A, iv - B

17. Jaundice is a disease of __________.
(A) Pancreas   (B) Liver
(C) Kidney   (D) Duodenum

18. AIDS is caused due to __________.
(A) Reduction to number of helper T-cells
(B) Auto immunity
(C) Non-production
(D) Reduction to number of killer T-cells

19. AIDS virus has __________.
(A) Single strand DNA
(B) Single strand RNA
(C) Double strand DNA
(D) Double strand RNA

20. TB is cured by __________.
(A) Encitol   (B) Ubiquinone
(C) Streptomycin   (D) Griseofuluin

21. Goitre is caused due to deficiency of __________.

(A) Fluorine   (B) Iodine
(C) Vitamin C   (D) Vitamin D

22. A chronic disease is __________.
(A) Hypertension   (B) Kala-azar
(C) Typhoid   (D) Diarrehoea

23. Droplet method of transmission of disease is found in __________.
(A) Syphilis   (B) AIDS
(C) Common cold   (D) Hepatitis

24. In chronic disease a patient suffers from __________.

(A) Tiredness
(B) Short breath
(C) Poor appetite
(D) All of these

25. Ascaris lumbricoides is common roundworm of __________.
(A) Bile duct
(B) Small intestine
(C) Large intestine
(D) Liver

26. Which one of the following diseases is not transmitted by mosquito?
(A) Dengue   (B) Brain fever
(C) Malaria   (D) Typhoid

27. Vectors can be defined as __________.
    (A) Microorganisms which cause many diseases
    (B) Animals carry the infecting agents from sick person to another healthy person.
    (C) Infected person
    (D) Diseased plants
28. Human disease caused by a bacterium is __________.
    (A) Polio   (B) Dengue
    (C) Tuberculosis   (D) Measles
29. Which one of the following has a long term effect on the health of an individual?
    (A) Stress
    (B) Common cold
    (C) Chicken pox
    (D) Chewing tobacco
30. Choose the wrong statement.
    (A) Acne is caused by staphylococci
    (B) Peptic ulcers are caused by eating acidic food
    (C) High blood pressure is caused by excessive weight and lack of exercise
    (D) Cancers can be caused by genetic abnormalities

HOTS (ACHIEVERS SECTION)

31. The coelom in arthropods is reduced and is known as 'haemocoel' because __________.
    (A) blood flows in the coelom.
    (B) coelom is filled with haemoglobin.
    (C) blood flows in the blood vessels present in the coelom.
    (D) coelomic fluid flows in the blood vessel.
32. Which of these statements listed below is true about common cold?
    (A) Common cold is not contagious.
    (B) Common cold virus can leave the body through the mucus of the infected people.
    (C) Common cold usually takes two months to clear up.
    (D) All of these
33. Anthrax is a ______ disease.
    (A) congenital   (B) genetic
    (C) infectious   (D) dangerous
34. The bacterium responsible for peptic ulcers is __________.
    (A) staphylococcus aureus
    (B) Helicobacter pylori
    (C) Streptococcus pneumonia
    (D) Nisseria
35. The diseases caused by defects that are present right from the birth are known as __________ diseases.
    (A) hereditary   (B) hormonal
    (C) genetic   (D) congenital

—Darken Your Choice with HB Pencil—

	A B C D		A B C D		A B C D		A B C D		A B C D
1.	Ⓐ Ⓑ Ⓒ Ⓓ	8.	Ⓐ Ⓑ Ⓒ Ⓓ	15.	Ⓐ Ⓑ Ⓒ Ⓓ	22	Ⓐ Ⓑ Ⓒ Ⓓ	29.	Ⓐ Ⓑ Ⓒ Ⓓ
2.	Ⓐ Ⓑ Ⓒ Ⓓ	9.	Ⓐ Ⓑ Ⓒ Ⓓ	16.	Ⓐ Ⓑ Ⓒ Ⓓ	23.	Ⓐ Ⓑ Ⓒ Ⓓ	30.	Ⓐ Ⓑ Ⓒ Ⓓ
3.	Ⓐ Ⓑ Ⓒ Ⓓ	10.	Ⓐ Ⓑ Ⓒ Ⓓ	17.	Ⓐ Ⓑ Ⓒ Ⓓ	24.	Ⓐ Ⓑ Ⓒ Ⓓ	31.	Ⓐ Ⓑ Ⓒ Ⓓ
4.	Ⓐ Ⓑ Ⓒ Ⓓ	11.	Ⓐ Ⓑ Ⓒ Ⓓ	18.	Ⓐ Ⓑ Ⓒ Ⓓ	25.	Ⓐ Ⓑ Ⓒ Ⓓ	32.	Ⓐ Ⓑ Ⓒ Ⓓ
5.	Ⓐ Ⓑ Ⓒ Ⓓ	12.	Ⓐ Ⓑ Ⓒ Ⓓ	19.	Ⓐ Ⓑ Ⓒ Ⓓ	26.	Ⓐ Ⓑ Ⓒ Ⓓ	33.	Ⓐ Ⓑ Ⓒ Ⓓ
6.	Ⓐ Ⓑ Ⓒ Ⓓ	13.	Ⓐ Ⓑ Ⓒ Ⓓ	20.	Ⓐ Ⓑ Ⓒ Ⓓ	27.	Ⓐ Ⓑ Ⓒ Ⓓ	34.	Ⓐ Ⓑ Ⓒ Ⓓ
7.	Ⓐ Ⓑ Ⓒ Ⓓ	14.	Ⓐ Ⓑ Ⓒ Ⓓ	21.	Ⓐ Ⓑ Ⓒ Ⓓ	28.	Ⓐ Ⓑ Ⓒ Ⓓ	35.	Ⓐ Ⓑ Ⓒ Ⓓ

NATURAL RESOURCES  14

LEARNING OBJECTIVES

➤ Environment
➤ The importance of air
➤ The importance of water

➤ Biogeochemical cycles
➤ The importance of ozone layer

MULTIPLE CHOICE QUESTIONS

1. The term used to identify the living components of the environment is __________.
   (A) Topographic
   (B) Ecosystem
   (C) Biotic
   (D) Abiotic

2. Air is a mixture of __________.
   (A) Nitrogen, oxygen, carbon monoxide, water vapours
   (B) Nitrogen, oxygen, carbon dioxide, water vapours
   (C) Nitrogen, carbon dioxide, oxygen, carbon monoioxide
   (D) Nitrogen, oxygen, methane, carbon dioxide

3. Which one is inexhaustible resource?
   (A) Soil
   (B) Solar radiation
   (C) Fossil fuels
   (D) Minerals

4. What is the range of temperature of the surface of moon?
   (A) –180°C to 100°C
   (B) –170°C to 100°C
   (C) –170°C to 120°C
   (D) –190°C to 110°C

5. The species of certain plants and animals which are present within certain region or area is called __________.
   (A) Phytoplankton
   (B) Biota
   (C) Kingdom
   (D) Zooplankton

6. Cloud formation takes place in which part of atmosphere __________.
   (A) Troposphere
   (B) Ozonosphere
   (C) Stratosphere
   (D) Thermosphere

7. Major component of the atmosphere on the Venus and Mars planets is __________.
   (A) Carbondioxide
   (B) Water vapours
   (C) Oxygen
   (D) Nitrogen

8. Biosphere occurs __________.
   (A) In atmosphere and hydrosphere
   (B) In lithosphere
   (C) In lithosphere and hydrosphere
   (D) At place of interatction of lithosphere, hydrosphere, hydrosphere and atmosphere.

9. All the elements of life support system are _________.
   (A) Inter connected
   (B) Inter related
   (C) Inter dependent
   (D) All of these

10. Percentage of total water found as fresh water is _________.
    (A) 32%   (B) 2.5%
    (C) 16%   (D) 46%

11. In a natural ecosystem, decomposers include _________.
    (A) Parasitic algae
    (B) Bacteria and fungi
    (C) Macroscopic animals
    (D) All of these

12. SPM includes _________.
    (A) Dust
    (B) Flyash
    (C) Soot and smoke
    (D) All of these

13. Photochemical smog is formed by _________.
    (A) CO   (B) SO_2
    (C) NO_2 (D) CO_2

14. Which of the following soils is the best for plant growth?
    (A) Sandy soil   (B) Loamy soil
    (C) Gravel   (D) Clay

15. In the atmosphere, the layer above the troposphere is _________.
    (A) Exosphere
    (B) Mesosphere
    (C) Stratosphere
    (D) Thermosphere

16. _________ is the major raw material for biogas.
    (A) Cow dung
    (B) Mud
    (C) Grass
    (D) Plant leaves

17. Biogas generation is mainly based on the principle of _________.
    (A) Degradation
    (B) Purification
    (C) Fermentation
    (D) Both (A) and (B)

18. Sanctuaries are established to _________.
    (A) Entrap animals
    (B) Protect animals
    (C) Rear animals for milk
    (D) None of these

19. The death of the last individual of a species is called _________.
    (A) Clad
    (B) Extinction
    (C) Neither (A) nor (B)
    (D) Species diversity

20. Red Data Book provides a list of _________.
    (A) Disease resistant animals
    (B) Advanced plants
    (C) Rare endangered or endemic species
    (D) None of these

21. Which of the following soils is transported by air?
    (A) Alluvial
    (B) Glacial
    (C) Aeolian
    (D) Elluvial

22. Green plants in an ecosystem are called _________.
    (A) Producers
    (B) Consumers
    (C) Decomposers
    (D) All of these

23. Signs of eutrophication of water bodies include _________.
    (A) Fluorosis
    (B) Algal bloom
    (C) Reduced oxygen
    (D) Rapid decomposition of organic matter

24. Match the column A with column B.

Column A	Column B
i. Hydrilla	a. Terrestrial
ii. Rat	b. Sea adaption
iii. Horse	c. Aquatic adaption
iv. Whale	d. Hydrophyte

(A) i – d, ii – a, iii – b, iv – c
(B) i – b, ii – a, iii – d, iv – c
(C) i – d, ii – a, iii – c, iv – b
(D) i – d, ii – c, iii – a, iv – b

25. Nif genes occur in __________.
(A) Aspergillus (B) Penicillium
(C) Rhizobium (D) Streptococcus

26. In nitrogen cycle which bacteria are responsible for nitrification?
(A) Rhizobium
(B) Clostridium
(C) Nitrosomonas
(D) Nitrosomonas and nitrobacter

27. The conversion of NO_3 to N_2 is called __________.
(A) Nitrification
(B) Denitrification
(C) Ammonifiction
(D) Nitrogen fixation

28. Nitromonas bacteria convert __________.
(A) Nitrite to nitrate
(B) Ammonia into nitrate
(C) Ammonia into nitrite
(D) Nitrite into ammonia

29. The two forms of oxygen found in the atmosphere are __________.
(A) Water and oxygen
(B) Water and ozone
(C) Water and carbon dioxide
(D) Ozone and oxygen

30. What would happen, if all land and water present in the environment is converted to ozone?
(A) We will be protected more
(B) Ozone is not stable, hence it will be toxic
(C) It will become poisonous and kill living forms
(D) It will help harmful sun radiations to reach earth and damage many life forms

HOTS (ACHIEVERS SECTION)

31. Identify the labelled parts P and R in the given cycle:

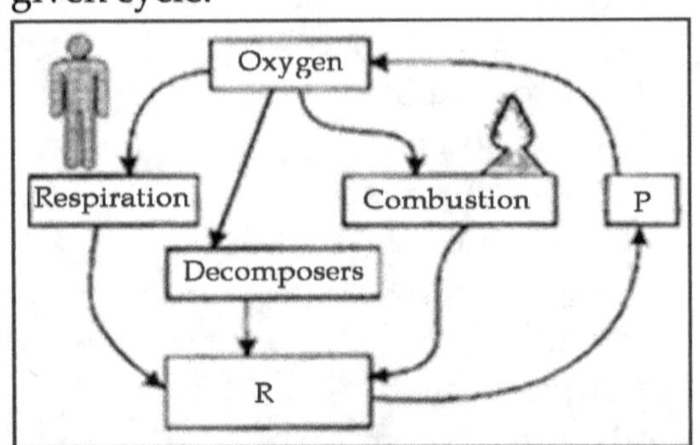

	P	R
(A)	Photosynthesis	Nitrogen
(B)	Respiration	Combustion
(C)	Excretion	Oxygen
(D)	Photosynthesis	Carbon dioxide

32. Which of the following cause greenhouse effect?
(i) Deforestation
(ii) Emission of gases from factories
(iii) Melting of polar ice
(A) Only (i) and (ii)
(B) Only (i) and (iii)
(C) Only (ii) and (iii)
(D) (i), (ii) and (iii)

33. Which of the following processes represents P, Q and R?

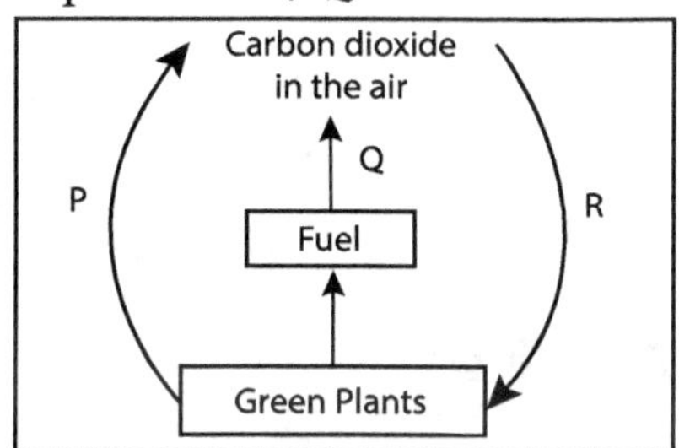

(A) P-Respiration, Q-Photosynthesis, R-Combustion
(B) P-Respiration, Q-Combustion, R-Photosynthesis
(C) P-Combustion, Q-Decay, R-Respiration
(D) P-Decay, Q-Respiration, R-Photosynthesis

34. Which of the following processes labelled with arrows are brought about by bacteria?

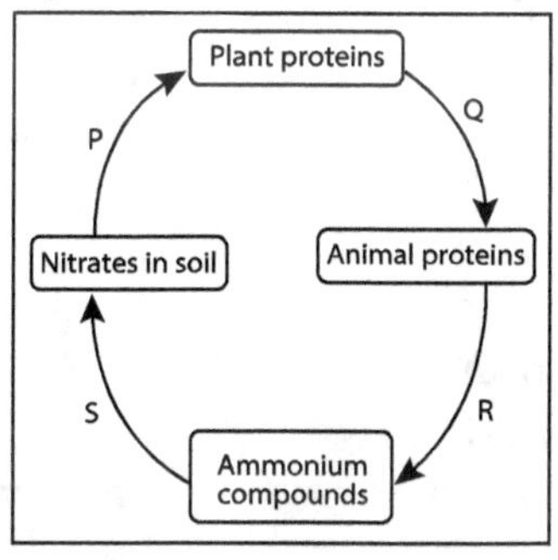

(A) P and Q   (B) Q and R
(C) R and S   (D) S and P

35. Which of the following processes represents X, Y and Z in the given cycle?

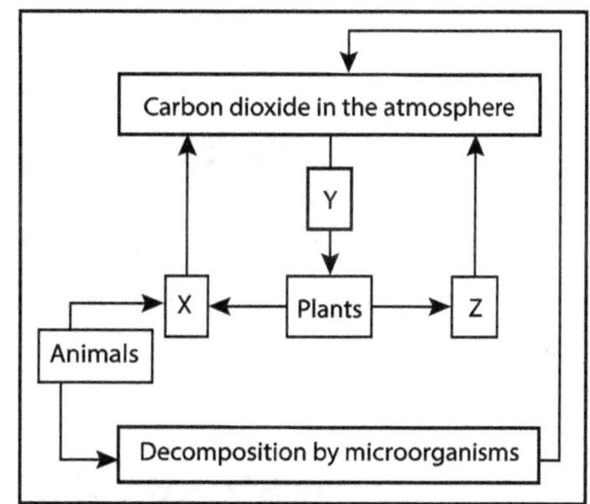

	X	Y	Z
(A)	Respiration	Photosynthesis	Decomposition
(B)	Photosynthesis	Respiration	Decomposition
(C)	Decomposition	Photosynthesis	Respiration
(D)	Decomposition	Respiration	Photosynthesis

—Darken Your Choice with HB Pencil—

IMPROVEMENT IN FOOD RESOURCES

MULTIPLE CHOICE QUESTIONS

1. Increase in oil production is __________.
   (A) White revolution
   (B) Blue revolution
   (C) Yellow revolution
   (D) Golden revolution

2. Organic farming does not include __________.
   (A) Crop rotation
   (B) Chemical fertilizers
   (C) Green manures
   (D) Compost and farmyard manures

3. The place for keeping and studying dry plants is called __________.
   (A) Museum
   (B) Vasculum
   (C) Arboreum
   (D) Herbarium

4. Which one of the following nutrients do we get from cereals?
   (A) Carbohydrates   (B) Vitamins
   (C) Proteins   (D) Minerals

5. Pulses are rich in __________.
   (A) Proteins
   (B) Oils
   (C) Vitamins and minerals
   (D) Carbohydrates

6. Which one is a micronutrient for the crop plants?
   (A) Potassium   (B) Iron
   (C) Magnesium   (D) Calcium

7. The technique used to obtain variety with high yield and other desirable characters is __________.
   (A) Hybridization
   (B) Selection
   (C) Introduction
   (D) Both (B) and (C)

8. Pusa lerma is an improved variety of __________.
   (A) Maize   (B) Wheat
   (C) Rice   (D) Soyabean

9. The botanical name of Dhaincha is __________.
   (A) Crotalaria
   (B) Trifolium alexandrium
   (C) Lens culinaris
   (D) Sesbania aculeata

10. The rust disease in wheat is caused by which one of the following microorganisms?
    (A) Puccinia   (B) Smut
    (C) Pyricularis   (D) Wachuria

11. Choose the complex fertilizer __________.
    (A) Triple super phosphate
    (B) Urea ammonium phosphate
    (C) Calcium ammonium nitrate
    (D) Potassium sulphate

12. Choose the abiotic factor __________.
    (A) Moisture content (B) Birds
    (C) Insects   (D) Fungi

13. All animals are __________.
    (A) Autotrophic   (B) Heterotrophic
    (C) Parasitic   (D) Saprophytic

14. The chief cereal crop of India is __________.
    (A) Maize   (B) Wheat
    (C) Sorghum   (D) Rice

15. Which is the most important source of food and fooder?
    (A) Cereal   (B) Fungi
    (C) Algae   (D) Lichen

16. Nodules with nitrogen-fixing bacteria are present in __________.
    (A) Wheat   (B) Cotton
    (C) Gram   (D) Mustrd

17. Gundhi bug is a pest of __________.
    (A) Wheat   (B) Rice
    (C) Maize   (D) Sorghum

18. Which of the following is not a sustainable agriculture technique?
    (A) Crop rotation
    (B) Mixed farming
    (C) Crop selection
    (D) Slash and burn farming

19. The element which is required in largest quantity by plants is __________.
    (A) Calcium   (B) Nitrogen
    (C) Sulphur   (D) Phosphorus

20. Application of nitrogen manure to a plant causes __________.
    (A) Early fruiting
    (B) Early flowering
    (C) Vigorous vegetative growth
    (D) Growth retardation due to toxicity

21. The lactation period for Red Sindhi is __________.
    (A) 230 to 394 days
    (B) 184 to 354 days
    (C) 250 to 410 days
    (D) 231 to 394 days

22. Who carried out the first experiment of artificial insemination?
    (A) Whitalker
    (B) John Dove
    (C) Spallanzani
    (D) Charles Martin

23. Find out the wrong statement from the following:
    (A) White revolution is meant for increase in milk production
    (B) Increasing food production without compromising with environment quality is called as sustainable agriculture.
    (C) Blue revolution is meant for increase in fish production
    (D) None of these

24. What is pulse rate of buffalo/minute?
    (A) 40 – 60/minutes
    (B) 70 – 72/minutes
    (C) 40 – 45/minutes
    (D) 16 – 18/minutes

25. Which of the poultry bird lays maximum number of eggs?
    (A) HH –260   (B) B –77
    (C) IBL –80   (D) ILS –82

26. Which of the following is not a draught animal?
    (A) Sheep   (B) Horse
    (C) Elephant   (D) Camel

27. Rotation of crops is essential for __________.
    (A) Increasing quality of proteins
    (B) Increasing fertility of soil
    (C) Increasing quality of minerals
    (D) Getting different kinds of crops

28. Which part of the plant breeding is an art?
   (A) Clonal selection
   (B) Pure line selection
   (C) Technique of hybridisation
   (D) Acclimatisation

29. Match the following.

i	White leghorn	a	Meat yielding poultry
ii	Karan swiss	b	Egg laying poultry
iii	Murrah	c	Buffalo
iv	Aseel	d	Exotic breed of cow

   (A) i –c, 2 –a, iii –d, iv –b
   (B) i –b, 2 –d, iii –c, iv –a
   (C) i –c, 2 –d, iii –a, iv –b
   (D) i –d, 2 –c, iii –b, iv –a

30. Which is the oldest breeding method?
   (A) Selection
   (B) Mutation
   (C) Hybridization
   (D) Introduction

HOTS (ACHIEVERS SECTION)

31. Select the correct match.

	Affected organism	Disease	Causal organism
(A)	Cattle	Anthrax	Bacteria
(B)	Poultry	Rinderpest	Virus
(C)	Cattle	Ranikhet	Virus
(D)	Poultry	Haemorrhagic septicaemia	Bacteria

32. Complete the given statements by selecting the correct words from the options given below.
   (A) ____(i)____ is a kind of manure which is prepared in the field itself to enrich soil with nitrogen and phosphorus.
   (B) ____(ii)____ is a draught breed of cattle.
   (C) In ____(iii)____ water escapes from revolving nozzle and falls like rain on the crops.
   (D) ____(iv)____ is the process of crossing individuals of two different species to produce hybrid.

	(i)	(ii)	(iii)	(iv)
(A)	Vermi compost	Malvi	Drip irrigation	Intravarietal hybridisation
(B)	Farm yard manure	Sahiwal	Chain pump	Intervarietal hybridisation
(C)	Compost	Gir	Moat	Intraspecific hybridisation
(D)	Green manure	Nageri	Sprinkler system	Interspecific hybridisation

33. Read the given statements.
   (i) Bee wax obtained from beehive is deposition of excretory products of honeybee.
   (ii) Fish culture is sometimes done in combination with rice crop so that fish are grown in the water accumulated in the paddy field.
   (iii) Fish feed in different zones of pond to make most efficient use of available food.
   (iv) Sahiwal and Murrah are exotic breeds used extensively in cattle farming.

(v) Intercropping is growing two or more crops simultaneously on the same field in a definite pattern.

Which of the given statements are incorrect?

(A) (i), (ii) and (iii) only
(B) (ii) and (iv) only
(C) (i) and (iv) only
(D) (i), (iv) and (v) only

34. Read the following statements (A–C) and select the option which correctly fills up the blanks in any two statements.

(A) ___(i)___ nutrients are required in large quantity and called as ___(ii)___.

(B) Kharif crops are cultivated from ___(iii)___ to ___(iv)___ .

(C) Berseem is an important ___(v)___ crop.

(A) (i) - 17, (ii) - Micronutrients, (iii) - June, (iv) - October
(B) (iii) - June, (iv) - October, (v) - Fodder
(C) (i) - 17, (ii) - Macronutrients, (v) - Field
(D) (iii) - November, (iv) - April, (v) - Rabi

35. The steps in the preparation of green manure are given below in a random order. Select the option that represents these steps in the correct sequence.

(A) Green plants are decomposed in soil.
(B) Quick growing green plants are cultivated.
(C) Plants are ploughed and mixed into the soil.
(D) After decomposition it becomes green manure.

(A) (C)→(B)→(A)→(D)
(B) (A)→(C)→(B)→(D)
(C) (A)→(B)→(C)→(D)
(D) (B)→(C)→(A)→(D)

	A B C D		A B C D		A B C D		A B C D		A B C D
1.	Ⓐ Ⓑ Ⓒ Ⓓ	8.	Ⓐ Ⓑ Ⓒ Ⓓ	15.	Ⓐ Ⓑ Ⓒ Ⓓ	22	Ⓐ Ⓑ Ⓒ Ⓓ	29.	Ⓐ Ⓑ Ⓒ Ⓓ
2.	Ⓐ Ⓑ Ⓒ Ⓓ	9.	Ⓐ Ⓑ Ⓒ Ⓓ	16.	Ⓐ Ⓑ Ⓒ Ⓓ	23.	Ⓐ Ⓑ Ⓒ Ⓓ	30.	Ⓐ Ⓑ Ⓒ Ⓓ
3.	Ⓐ Ⓑ Ⓒ Ⓓ	10.	Ⓐ Ⓑ Ⓒ Ⓓ	17.	Ⓐ Ⓑ Ⓒ Ⓓ	24.	Ⓐ Ⓑ Ⓒ Ⓓ	31.	Ⓐ Ⓑ Ⓒ Ⓓ
4.	Ⓐ Ⓑ Ⓒ Ⓓ	11.	Ⓐ Ⓑ Ⓒ Ⓓ	18.	Ⓐ Ⓑ Ⓒ Ⓓ	25.	Ⓐ Ⓑ Ⓒ Ⓓ	32.	Ⓐ Ⓑ Ⓒ Ⓓ
5.	Ⓐ Ⓑ Ⓒ Ⓓ	12.	Ⓐ Ⓑ Ⓒ Ⓓ	19.	Ⓐ Ⓑ Ⓒ Ⓓ	26.	Ⓐ Ⓑ Ⓒ Ⓓ	33.	Ⓐ Ⓑ Ⓒ Ⓓ
6.	Ⓐ Ⓑ Ⓒ Ⓓ	13.	Ⓐ Ⓑ Ⓒ Ⓓ	20.	Ⓐ Ⓑ Ⓒ Ⓓ	27.	Ⓐ Ⓑ Ⓒ Ⓓ	34.	Ⓐ Ⓑ Ⓒ Ⓓ
7.	Ⓐ Ⓑ Ⓒ Ⓓ	14.	Ⓐ Ⓑ Ⓒ Ⓓ	21.	Ⓐ Ⓑ Ⓒ Ⓓ	28.	Ⓐ Ⓑ Ⓒ Ⓓ	35.	Ⓐ Ⓑ Ⓒ Ⓓ

LOGICAL REASONING 

LEARNING OBJECTIVES

- ➤ Analogy
- ➤ Simple Analogy
- ➤ Classification
- ➤ Types of Series
- ➤ Concept of Coding and Decoding
- ➤ Number Test
- ➤ Time Sequence Test
- ➤ Concept of Alphabet Test
- ➤ Concept of Blood relation Test
- ➤ Concept of Mathematical Operations
- ➤ Types of Mathematical Operations
- ➤ Concept of Arithmetic Reasoning
- ➤ Types of Problems
- ➤ Concept of Inserting the missing character
- ➤ Problems based on continuation of figures
- ➤ Solving questions related to paper cutting
- ➤ Concept of Mirror Images
- ➤ Concept of Water Images
- ➤ Concept of Cubes and Dice

MULTIPLE CHOICE QUESTIONS

Directions (1–4): See the analogy given in the first pair of words and choose the correct option to establish the same relationship in the second pair.

1. Misogamy : Marriage : : Misogyny : ?
   - (A) Husband
   - (B) Women
   - (C) Relations
   - (D) Children

2. Coherent : Consistent : : Irate : ?
   - (A) Unhappy
   - (B) Irritated
   - (C) Angry
   - (D) Unreasonable

3. Skirmish : War : : Disease : ?
   - (A) Patient
   - (B) Medicine
   - (C) Infection
   - (D) Epidemic

4. Accomodation : Rent : : Journey : ?
   - (A) Octroi
   - (B) Fare
   - (C) Freight
   - (D) Expense

Directions (5–8): In each of the following questions four words have been given. Out of which three are alike in some manner, while the fourth one is different. Choose the odd one.

5. (A) Pallete
   (B) Trigger
   (C) Muzzle
   (D) Barrel

6. (A) Avalancle
   (B) Hurricane
   (C) Explosion
   (D) Earthquake

7. (A) Pepper
   (B) Cinnamon
   (C) Groundnut
   (D) Clove

8. (A) Dribble
   (B) Scoop
   (C) Bully
   (D) Bunker

Directions (9–12): There is a series of numbers which follow some definite order. Find the missing term and complete the series.

9. 3, 4, 5, 5, 12, 13, 7, 24, 25, 9, ?, 41
   (A) 40　　　　　　　(B) 35
   (C) 24　　　　　　　(D) 16

10. 1, 3, 6, 10, 15, 21, ?
    (A) 26　　　　　　　(B) 25
    (C) 28　　　　　　　(D) 30

11. 10, 17, 26, 37, 50, ?
    (A) 76　　　　　　　(B) 65
    (C) 95　　　　　　　(D) 84

12. 80, 63, 72, 72, 64, 81, 56, ?
    (A) 96　　　　　　　(B) 98
    (C) 89　　　　　　　(D) 90

13. In a certain code ZIP = 198, VIP = 222 then ZAP will be equal to _________.
    (A) 256　　　　　　　(B) 296
    (C) 246　　　　　　　(D) 276

14. In a certain system of coding, the word STATEMENT is written as TNEMETATS. In the same system of coding, what would be the code for the word POLITICAL?
    (A) LATILIOP　　　　(B) LCATILIOP
    (C) LACITILOP　　　(D) LCAITIOLP

15. In a certain code 134 means 'good and tasty', 478 means 'see good pictures' 728 means 'pictures are faint. Which of the following digit stands for pictures?
    (A) 4　　　　　　　　(B) 7
    (C) 8　　　　　　　　(D) 2

16. In a certain code, 'it be pee' means 'roses are blue', 'sik hee' means 'red flowers' and 'pee mit hee' means flowers are vegetables. How is 'red' written in that code?
    (A) hee　　　　　　　(B) be
    (C) sik　　　　　　　(D) pee

17. Raju is 5th from the left and Pankaj is 12th from the right end in a row of students. If Pankaj shifts three places towards Raju, his position is 10th from the left. How many students are there in the row?
    (A) 24　　　　　　　(B) 28
    (C) 26　　　　　　　(D) 27

18. If the day after tomorrow is Saturday. What day was three days before yesterday?
    (A) Monday　　　　　(B) Sunday
    (C) Friday　　　　　(D) Tuesday

19. In a particular year 1st November is Wednesday. What day was 1st October in that year?
    (A) Tuesday　　　　　(B) Sunday
    (C) Friday　　　　　(D) Monday

20. How many days will be there from 26th January 2008 to 15th may 2008 if both days are included?
    (A) 114　　　　　　　(B) 113
    (C) 117　　　　　　　(D) 111

21. If the English alphabet is written in reverse order then what will be the 4th letter to the right of 13th letter from the left?
    (A) G　　　　　　　　(B) J
    (C) L　　　　　　　　(D) K

22. If in the English alphabet, starting from 5th letter from the left, if 12 letters are written in reverse order then which letter will be 7th to the left of 14th letter from the right?
    (A) L　　　　　　　　(B) O
    (C) M　　　　　　　　(D) N

23. If 1st and 26th, 2nd and 25th, 3rd and 24th and so on, letters of English alphabet are paired then which of the following pairs is correct?
    (A) CW　　　　　　　(B) IP
    (C) GR　　　　　　　(D) EV

24. If the order of English alphabet is reversed which will be the 8th letter to the right of O?
    (A) W　　　　　　　　(B) V
    (C) G　　　　　　　　(D) E

25. Pointing towards Meena, Rajan said, "I am the only son of her mother's son." How is Meena related to Rajan?
    (A) Mother　　　　　(B) Aunt
    (C) Niece　　　　　　(D) Cousin

26. Introducing Rekha, Sarita said, "she is the only daughter of my father's only daughter." How is Sarita related to Rekha?

(A) Mother   (B) Niece

(C) Cousin   (D) Aunt

27. Pointing to Kanchan, Sulekha said, "He is the son of my father's only son." How is Kanchan mother related to Sulekha?

(A) Sister   (B) Aunt

(C) Daughter   (D) Sister-in-law

28. Mohan told Rajesh, "Yesterday I defeated the only brother of the daughter of my grandmother." Whom did Mohan defeat?

(A) Son   (B) Brother

(C) Father   (D) Cousin

29. If P means addition, Q means multiplication, R means division, S means subtraction, then what is the value of 4P10Q6R3S8?

(A) 34   (B) 24

(C) 16   (D) 8

30. If A denotes multiplication, B denotes addition, C denotes division and D denotes subtraction, then what is the value of 14A6B8C2D12?

(A) 76   (B) 86

(C) 82   (D) 72

31. If J stands for subtraction, K stands for multiplication, L stands for division and M stands for addition, then find the value of 27J15K2M18L3.

(A) 30   (B) 3

(C) 13   (D) 18

32. If × denotes −; ÷ denotes +, + denotes ÷ and − denotes ×, which one of the following equations is correct?

(A) $15 - 5 \div 5 \times 20 + 10 = 6$

(B) $8 \div 10 - 3 + 5 \times 6 = 8$

(C) $6 \times 2 + 3 \div 12 - 3 = 15$

(D) $3 \div 7 - 5 \times 10 + 3 = 10$

33. A certain number of horses and an equal number of men are going some where. Half of the men are on their horse's back while the remaining ones are walking along leading their horses. If the number of legs walking on the ground is 70. Find the number of horses.

(A) 16   (B) 10

(C) 14   (D) 12

34. Ram is three times as old as Mohan. Lokesh was twice as old as Ram four years ago. In four year's time Ram will be 31. What is the difference between present ages of Mohan and Lokesh?

(A) 41 years   (B) 36 years

(C) 37 years   (D) 40 years

35. Today is Mukesh's birthday. One year from today he will be twice as old as 12 years ago. What was the age of Mukesh 5 years ago?

(A) 20 years   (B) 25 years

(C) 30 years   (D) 15 years

36. Rajesh got twice as many sums wrong as he got right. If he attempted 84 sums in all. How many sums did he solve correctly?

(A) 24   (B) 28

(C) 26   (D) 32

Directions (37–40) Find the value of question mark (?) in the following questions:

37.

     9   25   4

1 (324) 81   16 (?) 1   64 (289) 16

    25   81   9

(A) 361   (B) 381

(C) 369   (D) 389

38.

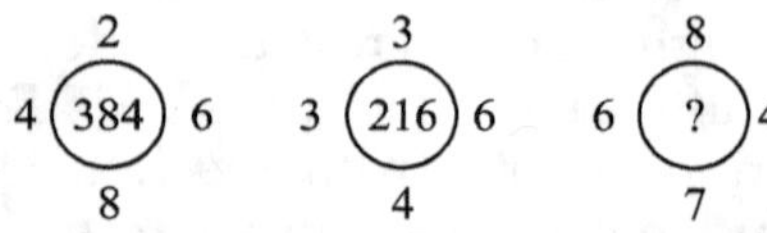

     2   3   8

4 (384) 6   3 (216) 6   6 (?) 4

    8   4   7

(A) 1344   (B) 1244

(C) 1342   (D) 1542

39. 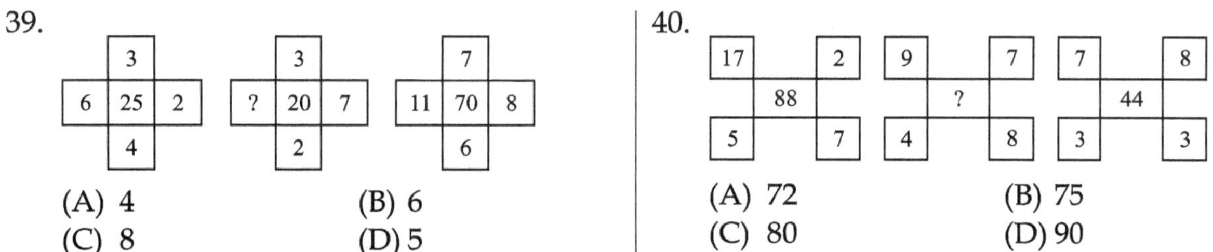

	3	
6	25	2
	4	

	3	
?	20	7
	2	

	7	
11	70	8
	6	

(A) 4   (B) 6

(C) 8   (D) 5

40.

(A) 72   (B) 75

(C) 80   (D) 90

Directions (41–44): Each of following questions consists of five figures marked A, B, C, D and E called the Problem Figures followed by five other figures marked a, b, c, d and e called the Answer Figures. Select a figure from amongst the Answer Figures which will continue the same series as established by the five Problem Figures.

Problem Figures	**Answer Figures**

41.

A   B   C   D   E   (A)   (B)   (C)   (D)   (E)

42.

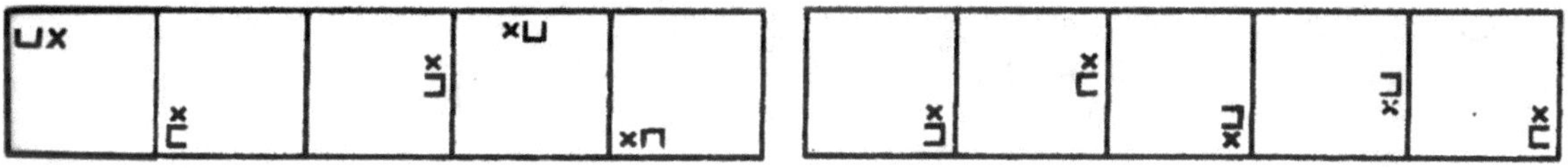

A   B   C   D   E   (A)   (B)   (C)   (D)   (E)

43.

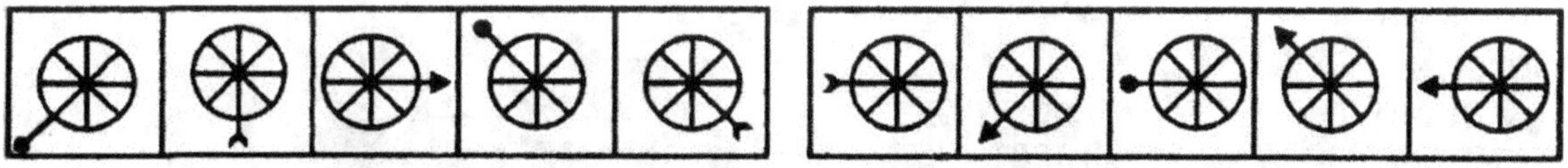

A   B   C   D   E   (A)   (B)   (C)   (D)   (E)

44.

A   B   C   D   E   (A)   (B)   (C)   (D)   (E)

Directions (45–48): In each of the following questions, a set of three figures X, Y, and Z have been given, showing a sequence in which a paper is folded and finally cut from a particular section. Below these figures a set of answer figures marked (a, b, c, d) showing the design which the paper actually acquires when it is unfolded are given. You have to select the answer figure which most closely resembles the unfolded piece of paper.

45.

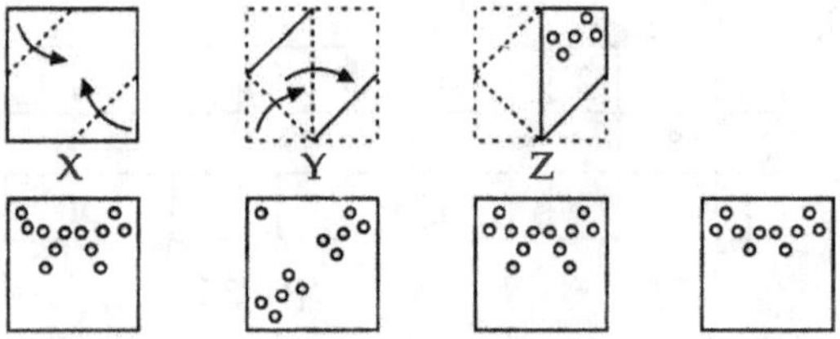

(A) (B) (C) (D)

46.

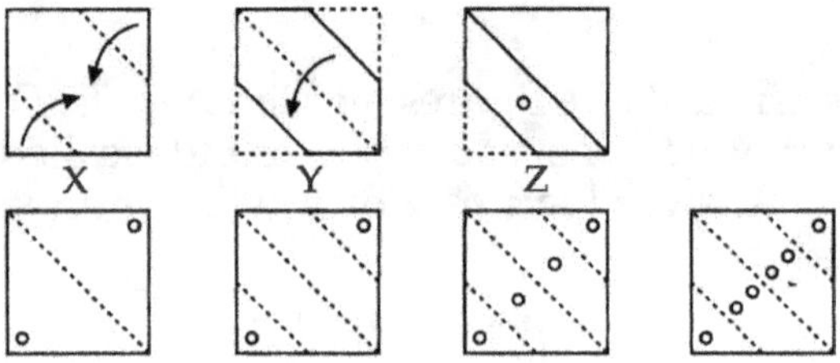

(A) (B) (C) (D)

47.

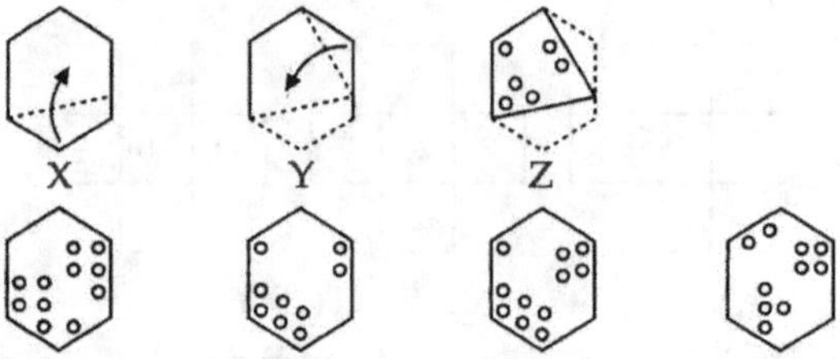

(A) (B) (C) (D)

48.

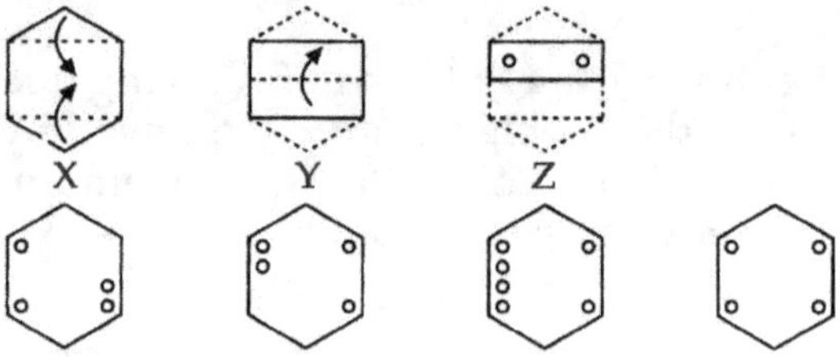

(A) (B) (C) (D)

Directions (49–52): Select one alternative which exactly matches with the mirror image of the word given in each question.

49. NIRMALA
(A) ALAMRIN (B) AJAMЯIИ
(C) NRILAMA (D) INRMALA

50. VINAYAKA
(A) INVAYAKA (B) AKAYANIV
(C) AꓘAYAИIV (D) NIVYAAKA

51. OBSTINATE
(A) ƎTAИITƧBO (B) BOSTINATE
(C) ETANITSBO (D) SOBTNIATE

52. PROCRASTINATE
(A) ETANITSARCORP (B) ƎTAИITƧAЯƆOЯꟼ
(C) RPORCASTNITAE (D) ETPROCRASTINA

Directions (53–56): In each of the following questions, a word is followed by four alternatives (A), (B), (C), (D) showing possible water images of that word. Choose the alternative which shows the correct water-image of that word.

53. CORDIAL
(A) LAIDROC (B) ꓶVIDꓤOC
(C) COꓤDIVꓶ (D) ꓶVIᗡꓤOƆ

54. PRECARIOUS
(A) ЬꓤECVꓤIOՈꙄ (B) PꓤECAꓤIOՈꙄ
(C) SUORECARIP (D) ƧUOIЯAƆƎЯꟼ

55. SUPERFLOUS
(A) SՈPERꟻLOՈS (B) SՈOꞀℲꓤƎdՈS
(C) ꙄՈЬEЯꟻꞀOՈꙄ (D) ꙄՈЬEꓤꟻꞀOՈꙄ

56. POLEMIC
(A) ƆIWƎꞀOꟼ (B) POLƎMIC
(C) ЬOꞀEWIC (D) ЬOꞀEMIↃ

Directions (57–60) Find the number of cubes in the following figures.

57.

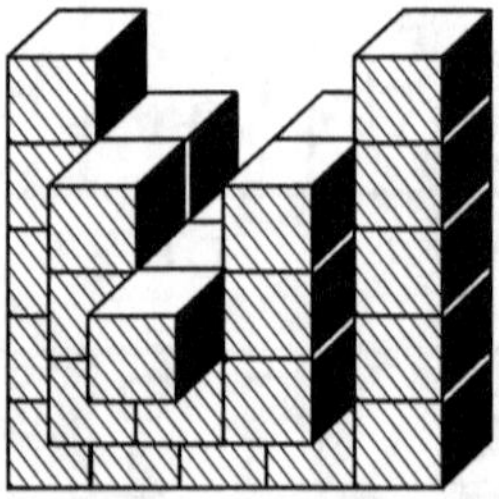

(A) 34 (B) 32 (C) 30 (D) 25

58.

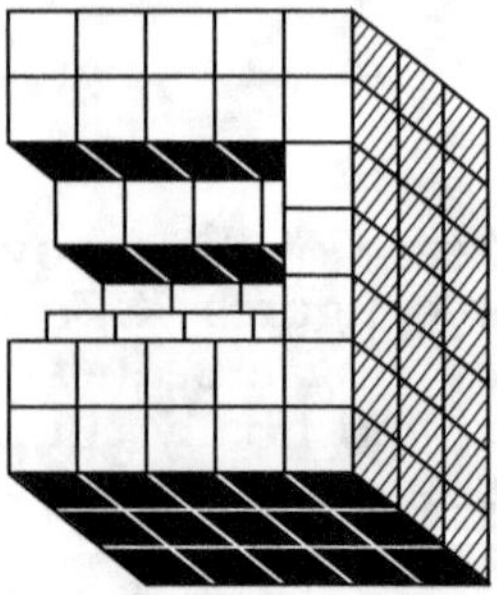

(A) 89 (B) 88 (C) 87 (D) 81

59.

(A) 150   (B) 168
(C) 158   (D) 144

60.

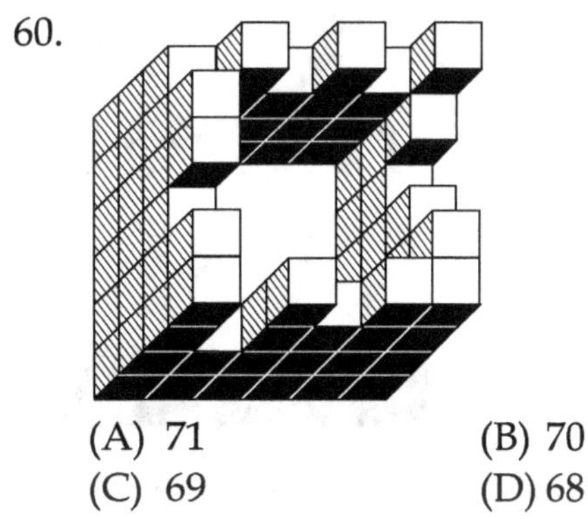

(A) 71   (B) 70
(C) 69   (D) 68

Darken Your Choice with HB Pencil

1. Ⓐ Ⓑ Ⓒ Ⓓ	13. Ⓐ Ⓑ Ⓒ Ⓓ	25. Ⓐ Ⓑ Ⓒ Ⓓ	37. Ⓐ Ⓑ Ⓒ Ⓓ	49. Ⓐ Ⓑ Ⓒ Ⓓ
2. Ⓐ Ⓑ Ⓒ Ⓓ	14. Ⓐ Ⓑ Ⓒ Ⓓ	26. Ⓐ Ⓑ Ⓒ Ⓓ	38. Ⓐ Ⓑ Ⓒ Ⓓ	50. Ⓐ Ⓑ Ⓒ Ⓓ
3. Ⓐ Ⓑ Ⓒ Ⓓ	15. Ⓐ Ⓑ Ⓒ Ⓓ	27. Ⓐ Ⓑ Ⓒ Ⓓ	39. Ⓐ Ⓑ Ⓒ Ⓓ	51. Ⓐ Ⓑ Ⓒ Ⓓ
4. Ⓐ Ⓑ Ⓒ Ⓓ	16. Ⓐ Ⓑ Ⓒ Ⓓ	28. Ⓐ Ⓑ Ⓒ Ⓓ	40. Ⓐ Ⓑ Ⓒ Ⓓ	52. Ⓐ Ⓑ Ⓒ Ⓓ
5. Ⓐ Ⓑ Ⓒ Ⓓ	17. Ⓐ Ⓑ Ⓒ Ⓓ	29. Ⓐ Ⓑ Ⓒ Ⓓ	41. Ⓐ Ⓑ Ⓒ Ⓓ	53. Ⓐ Ⓑ Ⓒ Ⓓ
6. Ⓐ Ⓑ Ⓒ Ⓓ	18. Ⓐ Ⓑ Ⓒ Ⓓ	30. Ⓐ Ⓑ Ⓒ Ⓓ	42. Ⓐ Ⓑ Ⓒ Ⓓ	54. Ⓐ Ⓑ Ⓒ Ⓓ
7. Ⓐ Ⓑ Ⓒ Ⓓ	19. Ⓐ Ⓑ Ⓒ Ⓓ	31. Ⓐ Ⓑ Ⓒ Ⓓ	43. Ⓐ Ⓑ Ⓒ Ⓓ	55. Ⓐ Ⓑ Ⓒ Ⓓ
8. Ⓐ Ⓑ Ⓒ Ⓓ	20. Ⓐ Ⓑ Ⓒ Ⓓ	32. Ⓐ Ⓑ Ⓒ Ⓓ	44. Ⓐ Ⓑ Ⓒ Ⓓ	56. Ⓐ Ⓑ Ⓒ Ⓓ
9. Ⓐ Ⓑ Ⓒ Ⓓ	21. Ⓐ Ⓑ Ⓒ Ⓓ	33. Ⓐ Ⓑ Ⓒ Ⓓ	45. Ⓐ Ⓑ Ⓒ Ⓓ	57. Ⓐ Ⓑ Ⓒ Ⓓ
10. Ⓐ Ⓑ Ⓒ Ⓓ	22. Ⓐ Ⓑ Ⓒ Ⓓ	34. Ⓐ Ⓑ Ⓒ Ⓓ	46. Ⓐ Ⓑ Ⓒ Ⓓ	58. Ⓐ Ⓑ Ⓒ Ⓓ
11. Ⓐ Ⓑ Ⓒ Ⓓ	23. Ⓐ Ⓑ Ⓒ Ⓓ	35. Ⓐ Ⓑ Ⓒ Ⓓ	47. Ⓐ Ⓑ Ⓒ Ⓓ	59. Ⓐ Ⓑ Ⓒ Ⓓ
12. Ⓐ Ⓑ Ⓒ Ⓓ	24. Ⓐ Ⓑ Ⓒ Ⓓ	36. Ⓐ Ⓑ Ⓒ Ⓓ	48. Ⓐ Ⓑ Ⓒ Ⓓ	60. Ⓐ Ⓑ Ⓒ Ⓓ

MODEL TEST PAPER

MULTIPLE CHOICE QUESTIONS

1. If the sum of four consecutive odd numbers is 40, the smallest number is ________
   (A) 7   (B) 9
   (C) 11   (D) 13

2. In the given figure, ABCD is a parallelogram. $DL \perp AB$ and $DM \perp BC$.

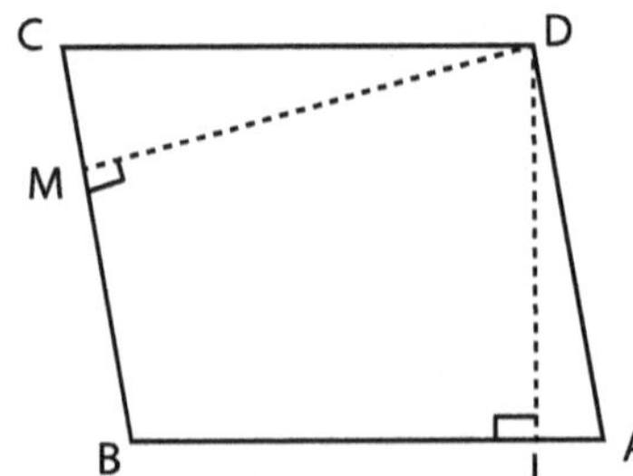

   If $AB = 18$ cm, $BC = 12$ cm and $DM = 10$ cm. Find DL.
   (A) 6 ½   (B) 6 cm
   (C) 6 cm   (D) None of these

3. Given that $4^{n+1} = 256$, find the value of n.
   (A) 2   (B) 3
   (C) 5   (D) 63

4. In the given figure, $AB \parallel CD$. Find the value of x.
   (A) 110°   (B) 120°
   (C) 130°   (D) 140°

5. The mean of 8 numbers is 25. If 5 is subtracted from each number, what will be the new mean?
   (A) 10   (B) 20
   (C) 30   (D) 40

6. In an examination, 96% of the candidates passed and 50 failed. How many candidates appeared in the examination?
   (A) 1240   (B) 1250
   (C) 1260   (D) 1270

7. In the given question, three classes are given. Out of the four figures that follow, you are to indicate which figure will best represent the relationship amongst the three classes.
   "Boys, Students, Athletes"

   (A) 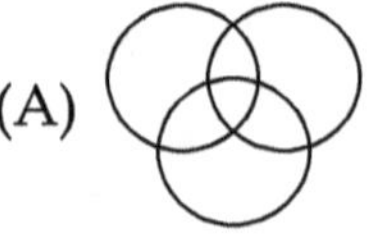   (B) 

   (C) 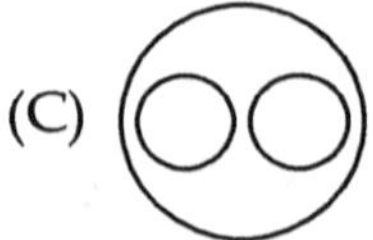   (D) 

8. Thirty six vehicles are parked in a parking lot in a single row. After the first car, there is one scooter. After the second car, there are two scooters. After the third car, there are three scooters and so on. Then the number of scooters in the second half of the row, is ________
   (A) 16   (B) 14
   (C) 15   (D) 13

9. Find the missing number in the given figure.

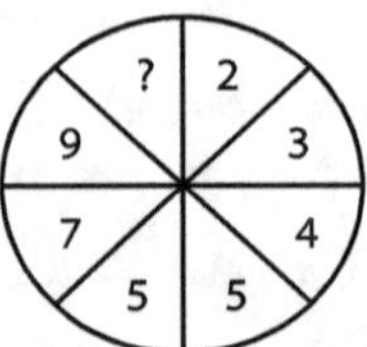

   (A) 10   (B) 11
   (C) 12   (D) 13

10. Count the number of triangles and squares in the given figure.

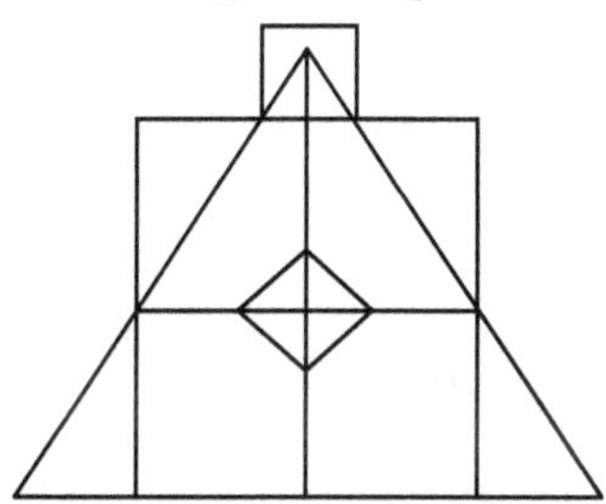

(A) 21 triangles, 7 squares
(B) 18 triangles, 8 squares
(C) 20 triangles, 8 squares
(D) 22 triangles, 7 squares

11. Find the next term in the series:

BMO, EOQ, HQS, ?

(A) KSU   (B) LMN
(C) SOV   (D) SOW

12. How many L's are there which do not have R preceding them and also do not have T following them?

Z Q S T L R M N Q N R T U V X R L T A
S L T Q R S L T

(A) 1   (B) 2
(C) 3   (D) 4

13. Eleven students *A, B, C, D, E, F, G, H, I, J* and *K* are sitting in the first line facing the teacher. *D* who is just to the left of *F*, is to the right of *C* at second place. *A* is second to the right of *E* who is at one end. *J* is the nearest neighbour of *A* and *B* and is to the left of *G* at third place. *H* is next to *D* to the right and is at the third place to the right of *I*. Who is just in the middle?

(A) *I*   (B) *B*
(C) *J*   (D) *G*

14. A new museum has two circular display rooms. The radius of the large circular room is 6 yards. The radius of the smaller circular room is 3 yards. What is the area of the smaller room in relation to the area of the large room?

(A) 1/6 of the large room's area
(B) 1/4 of the large room's area
(C) 1/3 of the large room's area
(D) 1/2 of the large room's area

15. If RAB = 36 and MEC = 195, then REG = __________.

(A) 240   (B) 160
(C) 40   (D) 630

16. Two bodies of equal masses (m) moving with equal velocities (v) in opposite directions collide. The resultant velocity of the combination is

(A) v   (B) 2v
(C) –v   (D) Zero

17. Which of the following distance time graphs does not represent a real situation?

(A)
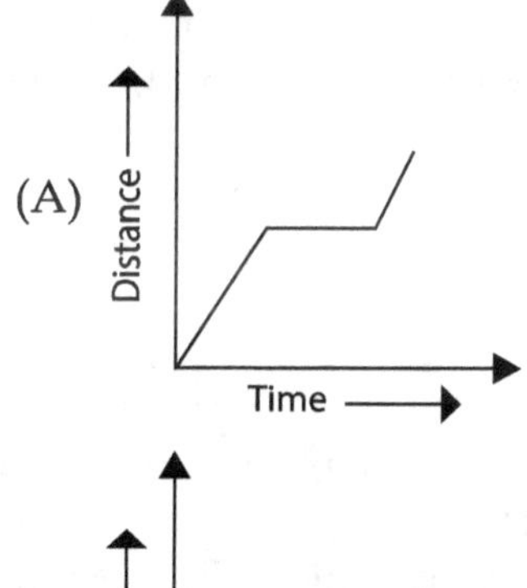

(B)
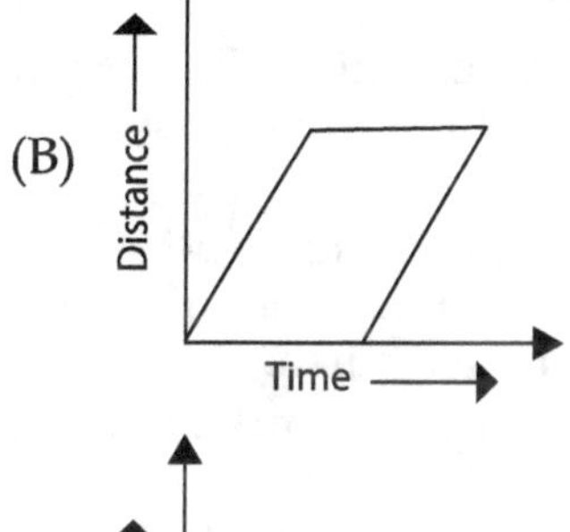

(C)
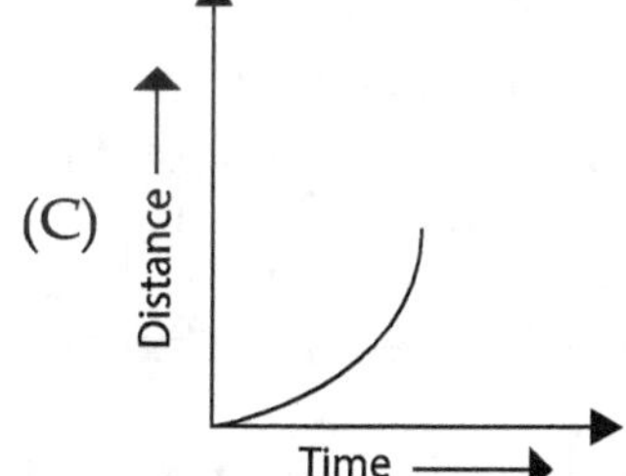

(D) 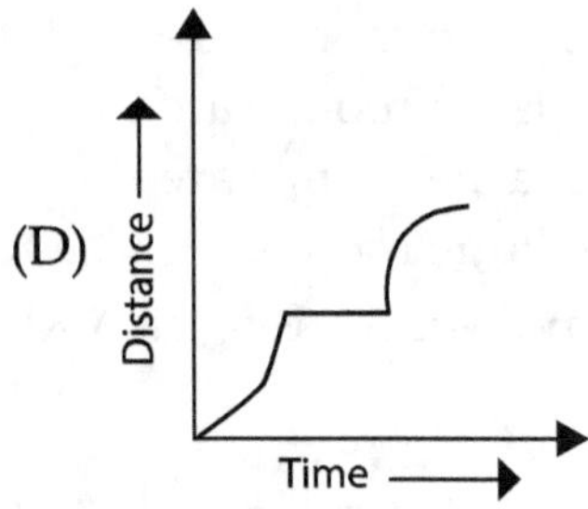

18. Which of the following is not an effect of inertia?
    (A) A person in a bus tends to fall backwards, when it starts suddenly.
    (B) When a tree is shaken vigorously, some of its leaves fall down.
    (C) A gun recoils back, when a bullet is fired from it.
    (D) None of these

19. A car and a motor cycle are moving with the same momentum. When equal retarding forces are applied, the car comes to halt in t_1 seconds and the motor cycle in t_2 seconds. If the mass of the car is five times more than the mass of the motor cycle, then __________
    (A) $t_1 = t_2$ (B) $t_1 = 1/5t_2$
    (C) $t_1 = t_2$ (D) $t_1 = 25t_2$

20. Read the given statements and choose the correct option.

    Statement 1: Acceleration due to gravity at a place on earth remains constant for all objects.

    Statement 2: Acceleration due to gravity doesn't depend on the mass of the object, but only on mass of earth.
    (A) Both statement 1 and statement 2 are true and statement 2 is correct explanation of statement 1.
    (B) Both statement 1 and statement 2 are true, but statement 2 is not correct explanation of statement 1.
    (C) Statement 1 is true but statement 2 is false.
    (D) Statement 1 is false but statement 2 is true.

21. Read the given statements and choose the correct option.

    Statement 1: There can be displacement of an object even in the absence of any force acting on it.

    Statement 2: An object in uniform motion in a straight line shows displacement even when the net force acting on it is zero.
    (A) Both statement 1 and statement 2 are true and statement 2 is correct explanation of statement 1.
    (B) Both statement 1 and statement 2 are true, but statement 2 is not correct explanation of statement 1.
    (C) Statement 1 is true but statement 2 is false.
    (D) Statement 1 is false but statement 2 is true.

Direction: Read the passage carefully and answer question numbers 22 and 23.

The relative density of a solid with respect to a liquid is 4/5 and relative density of the liquid with respect to water is 10/9. The buoyant force exerted by a liquid on a solid immersed in it is equal to the weight of the liquid displaced by the solid.

22. Specific gravity of solid with respect to water is
    (A) 18/25
    (B) 8/9
    (C) 0.56
    (D) 1.8

23. When 4 kg of this solid is immersed in water, the buoyant force experienced by it is (given $g = 9.8$ m s^{-2})
    (A) 4.5 g
    (B) 4 g
    (C) 5 g
    (D) 10 g

24. Match the following:

Column I	Column II
1. Paraffin wax	(p) Domestic fuel
2. Petrol	(q) Used for manufacturing steel
3. LPG	(r) Candles
4. Coke	(s) Aviation fuel

(A) 1 – (p); 2 – (q); 3 – (r); 4 – (s)
(B) 1 – (q); 2 – (p); 3 – (r); 4 – (s)
(C) 1 – (s); 2 – (r); 3 – (p); 4 – (q)
(D) 1 – (r); 2 – (s); 3 – (p); 4 – (q)

25. A spoon was kept in contact with ice cubes for some time. Later, the same spoon was held over the flame of a small candle. The figure shows the observation. What do you infer from the given figure?
(A) Spoon is an inflammable substance.
(B) Burning of candle is a spontaneous process.
(C) CO_2 is a product of combustion.
(D) Water vapour is a product of combustion.

26. Identify the incorrect statement from the given definitions of solids, liquids and gases in terms of melting and boiling points.
(A) A substance is said to be in solid state if under normal pressure, its melting point is above the room temperature.
(B) A substance is said to be in liquid state if under normal pressure, its melting point is below the room temperature.
(C) A substance is said to be in gaseous state if under normal pressure, its boiling point is below the room temperature.
(D) A substance can exist in solid, liquid and gaseous state under normal pressure and room temperature.

27. Membrane biogenesis is associated with which of the following cell organelles?

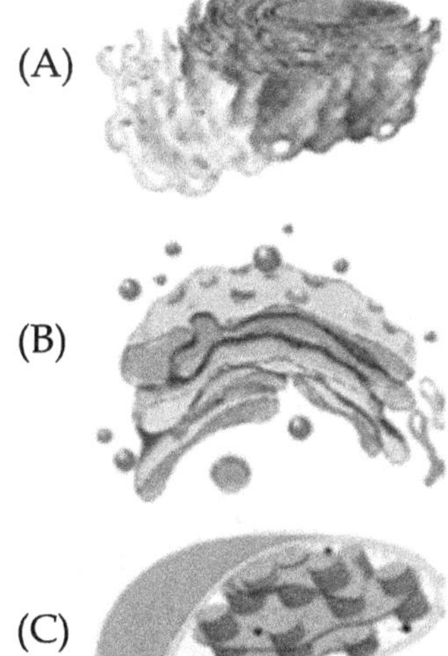

(A)

(B)

(C)

(D) Both (A) and (B)

28. Several microorganisms cause diseases in plants and reduce their yield. Which of the following plant diseases is incorrectly matched with its causal microorganism ?
(A) Citrus canker Bacteria
(B) Tobacco mosaic Virus
(C) Rust of wheat Fungi
(D) Yellow vein mosaic of bhindi Bacteria

29. ______ was the first one to observe free living cells. The term cell was given by ________. Cell theory was proposed by ________ and ________. All cells arise from preexisting cells was suggested by ________.

Select the correct sequence of names to complete the above paragraph.
(A) Robert Hooke, Virchow, Anton Von Leeuwenhoek, Schleiden, Schwann
(B) Anton Von Leeuwenhoek, Robert Hooke, Schleiden, Schwann, Virchow
(C) Robert Hooke, Virchow, Schleiden, Schwann, Anton Von Leeuwenhoek
(D) Anton Von Leeuwenhoek, Virchow, Schleiden, Schwann, Robert Hooke

30. Which of the following diseases is not transmitted by the vector shown in the figure?

(i)   Malaria   (ii) Yellow fever
(iii) Typhoid   (iv) Sleeping sickness
(v)   Kalaazar

(A) (ii), (iii) and (iv)
(B) (i), (iii) and (v)
(C) (i) and (ii)
(D) (iii), (iv) and (v)

31. A __(i)__ is a nonliving, elongated cell with tapering ends. Its walls are highly thickened with __(ii)__ except at certain circular spots known as __(iii)__. A __(iv)__ is a cylindrical tubelike structure placed one above the other end to end. ____(v)____ is a nonliving, thick walled cell providing mechanical support.

Select the correct sequence of words to complete the above paragraph.

	(A)	(B)	(C)	(D)
(i)	Vessel	Tracheid	Vessel	Tracheid
(ii)	Lignin	Suberin	Suberin	Lignin
(iii)	Stoma	Pits	Stoma	Pits
(iv)	Tracheid	Vessel	Tracheid	Vessel
(v)	Xylem fibre	Parenchyma	Sclereid	Xylem fibre

32. Which of the following are threatened wild animals?

(i)   Golden cat   (ii) Pink hued duck
(iii) Dinosaur   (iv) Dodo
(v)   Passenger   (vi) White tailed
      pigeon   mongoose
(vii) Gharial   (viii) Marsh crocodile

(A) (i), (ii), (iv) and (v)
(B) (v), (vi), (vii) and (viii)
(C) (ii), (iv), (vi) and (vii)
(D) (i), (ii), (vii) and (viii)

Direction: Refer the given experiment and answer Q. nos. 33 and 34.

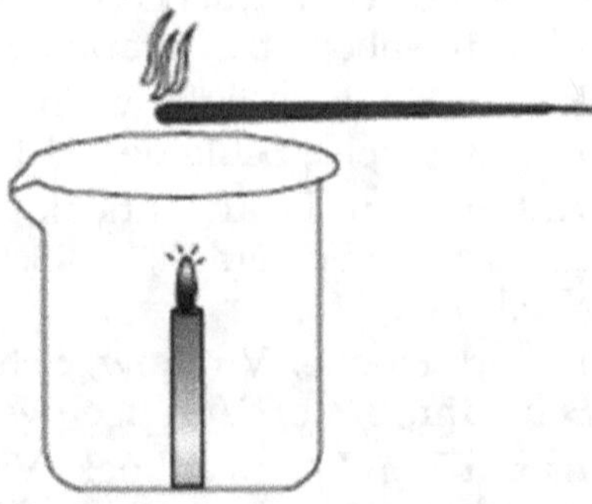

Place a candle in a beaker or a widemouthed bottle and light it. Light an incense stick (agarbati) and take it to the mouth of the beaker as shown in figure. Note the way in which the smoke flows when the incense stick is (i) near the edge of the beaker, (ii) kept a little above the candle, and (iii) kept in other regions.

33. In which case, the direction of flow of smoke will be towards the candle first and then upwards?

(A) (i)
(B) (ii)
(C) (iii)
(D) Both (i) and (iii)

34. What does the above experiment show?

(A) The direction of movement of hot and cold air.
(B) Oxygen is present in the air and is necessary for burning.
(C) The temperature of air inside the bottle is more than the temperature of open air.
(D) The direction in which the maximum smoke is produced & pollutes the environment.

35. This implement is made of wood and is drawn by a pair of bulls or other animals. It contains a strong triangular iron strip called share. The main part of it is a long log of wood which is called a shaft. There is a handle at one end of the shaft. The other end is attached to a beam which is placed on the bulls' necks.

Which implement are we talking about and for what purpose is it used?

(A) Plough Tilling the soil

(B) Hoe Removing the weeds

(C) Cultivator Sowing the seeds

(D) Seed drill Tilling the soil

36. In honey bee the drones (males) are produced from

(A) Unfertilized eggs

(B) Fertilized eggs

(C) Larvae from unfertilized eggs, which are fed on royal jelly

(D) Larvae from unfertilized eggs, which are not cared by the workers at all

37. A sonic 'tape measure' is used to measure the length of a room. It measures a time interval of 0.06 s between transmitting a sound pulse and receiving the echo. The speed of sound in air is 330 m/s. How far is the reflecting wall from the tape measure?

(A) 5.5 m

(B) 9.9 m

(C) 11 m

(D) 20 m

38. A person exerts a horizontal force of 500 N on a box, which also experiences a frictional force of 100 N. How much work is done against friction when the box moves a horizontal distance of 3 m?

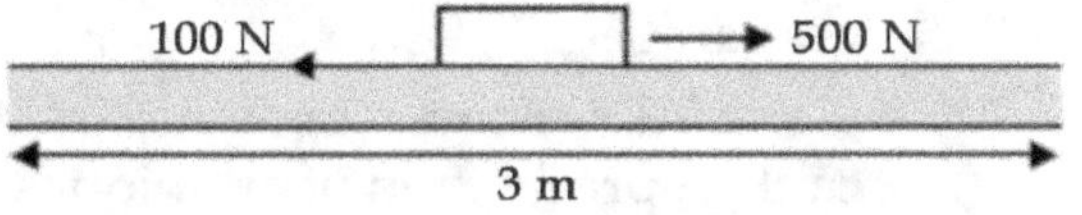

(A) 300 J

(B) 1200 J

(C) 1500 J

(D) 1800 J

39. Thermometer X at 20°C is placed in some water at 50°C in beaker Y. After some time, thermometer X will show a maximum temperature of _____.

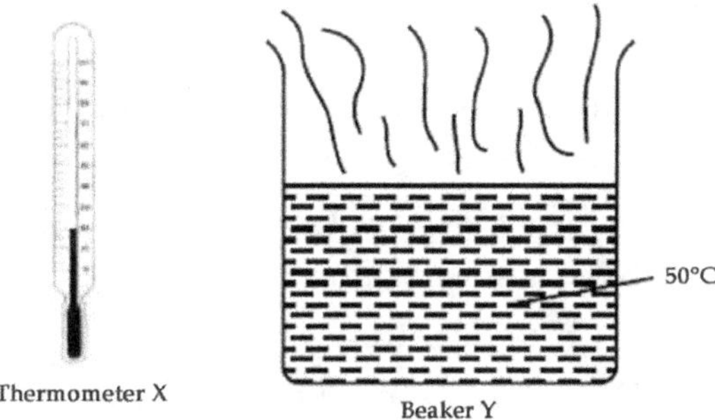

(A) 20°C

(B) 35°C

(C) 50°C

(D) 30°C

40. The experiment given below shows that light _____________.

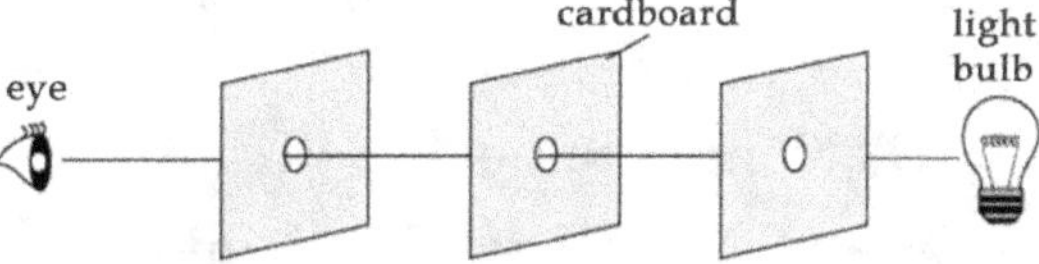

(A) Can be reflected

(B) Is a form of energy

(C) Travels in straight line

(D) Can pass through all objects

41. When we remove polyester or woolen cloth in dark, we can see sparks and hear a cracking sound. These are due to ___________.

(A) Static electricity

(B) Current electricity

(C) Reflection of light

(D) Refraction of light

42. A car starts from rest and is uniformly accelerated to a speed of 30 m/s in 6 s. What is the distance travelled by the car?

(A) 5 m

(B) 30 m

(C) 90 m

(D) 180 m

43. A crane uses a petrol engine to lift a heavy girder. What is the overall energy conversion in the system when the girder is moving at a steady rate?

(A) Chemical into kinetic

(B) Chemical into potential

(C) Kinetic into potential

(D) Potential into kinetic

44. Solids cannot be compressed because ______.

(A) The constituent particles are closely packed

(B) The movement of the constituent particles is restricted

(C) The intermolecular attractive forces are very strong

(D) None of these

45. X and Y are miscible liquids. Boiling point of X is 56°C and that of Y is 100°C. Which separation technique can be used to separate X and Y from the mixture?

(A) Separating funnel

(B) Distillation

(C) Evaporation

(D) Condensation

46. The solubility of potassium chloride at 20°C is 34.7 g in 100 g of water. The density of the solution is 1.3 g mL^{-1}. What is the w/V percentage of potassium chloride in the solution?

(A) 25.76   (B) 32.98

(C) 33.49   (D) 22.56

47. What will be the number of aluminium ions in 0.051 g of aluminium oxide?

(A) 5.0×10^{-4} ions

(B) 6.0×10^{23} ions

(C) 12×10^{23} ions

(D) 6.0×10^{20} ions

48. An ion M^{2+} contains 10 electrons and 12 neutrons. What is the atomic number and mass number of element M?

(A) 10, 24

(B) 10, 22

(C) 12, 24

(D) 12, 22

49. Microorganisms are our friends and foes. Some of them are useful for us while some of them are harmful. From the given list sort out useful and harmful actions of microorganisms. Production of antibiotics, food spoiling, curd preparation, vaccine production, citrus canker.

(A) Useful: Curd preparation, citrus canker, production of antibiotics.
Harmful: Food spoiling, vaccine production.

(B) Useful: Production of antibiotics, curd preparation, vaccine production.
Harmful: Food spoiling, citrus canker.

(C) Useful: Citrus canker, vaccine production, curd preparation.
Harmful: Food spoiling, production of antibiotics

(D) Useful: Vaccine production, curd preparation.
Harmful: Food spoiling, citrus canker, production of antibiotics.

50. A layer of air known as the atmosphere surrounds the earth. The composition of the atmosphere can be changed by air pollution. Which of the following statements about air pollution are correct?

(i) It affects the weather.

(ii) It covers the leaves of plants and limits photosynthesis.

(iii) It may cause breathing difficulties and diseases of the respiratory tract.

(iv) It is mostly caused by the burning of fossil fuels.

(A) (iii) & (iv)

(B) (i), (ii) & (iii)

(C) (i), (iii) & (iv)

(D) (i), (ii), (iii) & (iv)

1.	Ⓐ Ⓑ Ⓒ Ⓓ	11.	Ⓐ Ⓑ Ⓒ Ⓓ	21.	Ⓐ Ⓑ Ⓒ Ⓓ	31	Ⓐ Ⓑ Ⓒ Ⓓ	41.	Ⓐ Ⓑ Ⓒ Ⓓ
2.	Ⓐ Ⓑ Ⓒ Ⓓ	12.	Ⓐ Ⓑ Ⓒ Ⓓ	22.	Ⓐ Ⓑ Ⓒ Ⓓ	32.	Ⓐ Ⓑ Ⓒ Ⓓ	42.	Ⓐ Ⓑ Ⓒ Ⓓ
3.	Ⓐ Ⓑ Ⓒ Ⓓ	13.	Ⓐ Ⓑ Ⓒ Ⓓ	23.	Ⓐ Ⓑ Ⓒ Ⓓ	33.	Ⓐ Ⓑ Ⓒ Ⓓ	43.	Ⓐ Ⓑ Ⓒ Ⓓ
4.	Ⓐ Ⓑ Ⓒ Ⓓ	14.	Ⓐ Ⓑ Ⓒ Ⓓ	24.	Ⓐ Ⓑ Ⓒ Ⓓ	34.	Ⓐ Ⓑ Ⓒ Ⓓ	44.	Ⓐ Ⓑ Ⓒ Ⓓ
5.	Ⓐ Ⓑ Ⓒ Ⓓ	15.	Ⓐ Ⓑ Ⓒ Ⓓ	25.	Ⓐ Ⓑ Ⓒ Ⓓ	35.	Ⓐ Ⓑ Ⓒ Ⓓ	45.	Ⓐ Ⓑ Ⓒ Ⓓ
6.	Ⓐ Ⓑ Ⓒ Ⓓ	16.	Ⓐ Ⓑ Ⓒ Ⓓ	26.	Ⓐ Ⓑ Ⓒ Ⓓ	36.	Ⓐ Ⓑ Ⓒ Ⓓ	46.	Ⓐ Ⓑ Ⓒ Ⓓ
7.	Ⓐ Ⓑ Ⓒ Ⓓ	17.	Ⓐ Ⓑ Ⓒ Ⓓ	27.	Ⓐ Ⓑ Ⓒ Ⓓ	37.	Ⓐ Ⓑ Ⓒ Ⓓ	47.	Ⓐ Ⓑ Ⓒ Ⓓ
8.	Ⓐ Ⓑ Ⓒ Ⓓ	18.	Ⓐ Ⓑ Ⓒ Ⓓ	28.	Ⓐ Ⓑ Ⓒ Ⓓ	38.	Ⓐ Ⓑ Ⓒ Ⓓ	48.	Ⓐ Ⓑ Ⓒ Ⓓ
9.	Ⓐ Ⓑ Ⓒ Ⓓ	19.	Ⓐ Ⓑ Ⓒ Ⓓ	29.	Ⓐ Ⓑ Ⓒ Ⓓ	39.	Ⓐ Ⓑ Ⓒ Ⓓ	49.	Ⓐ Ⓑ Ⓒ Ⓓ
10.	Ⓐ Ⓑ Ⓒ Ⓓ	20.	Ⓐ Ⓑ Ⓒ Ⓓ	30.	Ⓐ Ⓑ Ⓒ Ⓓ	40.	Ⓐ Ⓑ Ⓒ Ⓓ	50.	Ⓐ Ⓑ Ⓒ Ⓓ

HINTS AND SOLUTIONS

1. MATTER IN OUR SURROUNDINGS

Answer Key

1. (A)	2. (B)	3. (A)	4. (B)	5. (B)	6.(A)	7. (D)	8. (B)	9. (D)	10. (A)
11. (C)	12. (B)	13. (B)	14. (B)	15. (A)	16. (A)	17. (D)	18. (B)	19. (B)	20. (B)
21. (B)	22. (C)	23. (A)	24. (D)	25. (C)	26. (A)	27. (C)	28. (B)	29. (B)	30. (B)

3. (A)

Temperature on Kelvin scale = Temperature on Celsius scale + 273

(i) = 0 + 273

= 273 K

(ii) = -6 + 273

= 267 K

(iii) = 273 + 273

= 546 K

13. (B)

Temperature on Kelvin scale = Temperature on Celsius scale + 273

(i) Temperature on Celsius scale = 308 - 273

(i) = 35°C

(ii) = 329 - 273

= 56°C

(iii) = 391 - 273

= 118°C

15. (A)

Temperature on Celsius scale = Temperature on Kelvin scale + 273

= 268 - 273

= -5°C

16. (A)

Temperature on Kelvin scale = Temperature on Celsius scale + 273

= -88 + 273

= 185 k

28. (B)

Temperature on Celsius scale = Temperature on Kelvin scale - 273

= 300 − 273

= 27°C

HOTS (ACHIEVERS SECTION)

31. (B)	32. (B)	33. (C)	34. (A)	35. (D)

OLYMPIAD WORKBOOK (NSO) CLASS— 9

Answer Key

1. (B)	2. (B)	3. (A)	4. (C)	5. (B)	6.(C)	7. (B)	8. (B)	9. (B)	10. (B)
11. (C)	12. (A)	13. (A)	14. (C)	15. (D)	16. (A)	17. (B)	18. (A)	19. (C)	20. (B)
21. (A)	22. (D)	23. (A)	24. (B)	25. (D)	26. (B)	27. (A)	28. (C)	29. (D)	30. (A)

8. (B)

Concentration of solution

$$= \frac{\text{mass solute}}{\text{mass of solution}} \times 100$$

$$= \frac{10}{160} \times 100 = \frac{100}{16}$$

$$= 6.25\%$$

19. (C)

Concentration of solution

$$= \frac{\text{mass solute}}{\text{mass of solution}} \times 100$$

Mass of solute (salt) = 80 g

Mass of solution = 80 + 500 = 580

$$= \frac{80}{580} \times 100$$

$$= 13.793$$

Or

$$= 13.8\%$$

HOTS (ACHIEVERS SECTION)

31. (C)	32. (C)	33. (B)	34. (D)	35. (C)

33. (B)

Emperical formula = CH_2O

Emperical formula weight

$= 12 + 12 + 16 = 30$

$$N = \frac{\text{molecular weight}}{\text{emperical formula weight}} \frac{90}{30} = 3$$

Thus, molecular formula of $(CH_2O)_3$

$= C_3H_6O_3.$

Answer Key

1. (B)	2. (C)	3. (A)	4. (B)	5. (C)	6. (B)	7.(C)	8. (D)	9. (B)	10. (D)
11. (B)	12. (D)	13. (A)	14. (C)	15. (B)	16. (A)	17. (B)	18. (B)	19. (A)	20. (B)
21. (C)	22. (B)	23. (B)	24. (B)	25. (C)	26. (A)	27. (B)	28. (D)	29. (C)	30. (A)

6. (B)

$H_2O = 2 : 16 = 1 : 8$

7. (C)

Gram molecular weight of $Pb(NO_3)_2$

$= 207 + (2 \times 14) + 2(16 \times 3)$

$= 207 + 28 + 96 = 331$

1 mole of $Pb(NO_3)_2$ is 331g

Therefore, 0.2 mole of $Pb(NO_3)_2$ is

331×0.2

$= 66.2$ g

8. (D)

Molecular weight of $Mg(NO_3)_2 \cdot 6H_2O$

$= 24 + 2(14 + 16 \times 3) + 6(2 \times 1 + 16)$

$= 24 + 124 + 108 = 256$ amu

Atomic mass of oxygen in $Mg(NO_3)_2 \cdot 6H_2O$ is,

$= 2(16 \times 3 \times 6(16) = 96 + 96 = 192$

% of oxygen $= \dfrac{192}{256} \times 100 = 75\%$

10. (D)

$X \rightarrow X^{3+}$ means it loses three electrons, so

$X^{3+} = 10$ electrons

13. (A)

$Z \rightarrow Z^{3-}$ means it gains three electrons

Atomic number = no. of electrons.

So, the atomic number of element Z is $= 7$

14. (c)

Gram molecular weight of $NH_3 = 14 + (1 \times 3)$

$= 17$ g

17 g of $NH_3 = 22.4$ litres

$\therefore \quad 3.4 \times 10^3$g of NH $= \dfrac{22.4}{17} \times 3.4 \times 10^3$

$= \dfrac{76160}{17} = 4480$ litres

17. (B)

No. of electron = No. of proton but in this case electron is less than proton. In cation also less electrons are present than a neutral atom.

19. (A)

Formula : X_3Y

Symbol   X   Y

Valencies 1   3

20. (B)

mole of $FeSO_4 \cdot 7H_2O$ = Formula mass of $FeSO_4 \cdot 7H_2O$ in grams

= Mass of Fe + Mass of S + Mass of O $\times$ 11 + mass of H $\times$ 14

$= 56 + 32 + 16 \times 11 + 1 \times 14$

$= 278$ g

21. (C)

$1\,(Ca) + 2\,(Cl) = 40 + 2 \times 35.5 = 111$ amu

22. (B)

1 atom of element Z has mass $= 2.65 \times 10^{-23}$ g

Hence 6.023×10^{23} atoms of element Z have mass

$= 2.65 \times 10^{-23} \times 6.023 \times 10^{23}$

$= 15.69$ g

27. (B)

We know that

6.022×10^{23} molecules of sulphur dioxide

$= 1$ mole

So, 12.044×10^{23} molecules of sulphur dioxide

$= \dfrac{1}{6.022 \times 10^{23}} \times 12.044 \times 10^{22}$

$= \dfrac{2}{10} = 0.2$ mole

28. (D)

Element	% Weight	Atomic Weight	Relative Number of Atoms	Simplest Ratio of Atoms
H	2.04	1	2.04/1 = 2.04	2.04/1.02 = 2
S	32.65	32	32.65/32 = 1.02	1.02/1.02 = 1
O	65.31	16	65.31/16 = 4.08	4.08/1.02 = 4

Empirical formula is H_2SO_4

Empirical formula mass

$= (2 \times 1) + 32 + (16 \times 4)$

$= 98$

Relative molecular mass = 98

$$n = \frac{\text{Relative molecular mass}}{\text{Empirical formula mass}} = \frac{98}{98} = 1$$

$\therefore$ Molecular formula $= n \times$ Empirical formula

$= 1 \times H_2SO^4 = H_2SO_4$

30. (A)

1 mole of atoms contain 6.022×10^{23} atoms

$\because$ 1 mole of sodium atoms $= 6.022 \times 10^{23}$ atoms

$\therefore$ 0.2 mole of sodium atoms $= 6.022 \times 10^{23} \times 0.2$ atoms

$= 12.044 \times 10^{22}$ atoms

HOTS (ACHIEVERS SECTION)

31. (C)	32. (A)	33. (B)	34. (A)	35. (C)

4. STRUCTURE OF ATOM

Answer Key

1. (B)	2. (B)	3. (D)	4. (D)	5. (C)	6. (C)	7. (D)	8.(C)	9. (C)	10 (B)
11. (B)	12. (B)	13. (A)	14. (A)	15. (D)	16. (B)	17. (B)	18. (D)	19. (D)	20. (B)
21. (C)	22. (A)	23. (C)	24. (A)	25. (B)	26. (D)	27. (C)	28. (B)	29. (A)	30. (B)

9. (C)

Number of electron = Number of proton

= Number of atomic Number

i.e., Number of proton = 15

Number of neutron = 16

Therefore mass number

= Number proton + Number of neutron

$= 15 + 16 = 31$

Mass number

Symbol of element i.e., $^{31}_{15}X$

Atomic number

13. (A)

The atomic number of S = 6

In sulphide ion S^{2-} means it acquires this configuration by gaining two electrons. Means the valence electron is (8).

16. (B)

Isobar means same mass number but different atomic numbers.

17. (B)

Cation means it loses electron but electronic configuration of $_{12}A$ is 2, 8, 2, $_{13}B$ is 2, 8, 3 $_{15}C$ is 2, 8, 5 and $_3D$ is 2, 1 Elements A, B, and D easily lose electron and acquire positive charge but element C for acquiring stable configuration gains 3 electrons instead of losing five electrons and form an anion.

21. (C)

Number of neutron = mass number – proton number.

$= 23 - 11 = 12$

22. (A)

Number of electron = Mass Number – neutron number.

$= 27 - 14 = 13$

But element has 3 positive charge it means it loses 3 electrons. So the no. of electron is 10.

23. (C)

Electronic configuration of $_{17}Cl$ atom is = 2, 8, 7

Electronic configuration of Cl^- ion is = 2, 8, 8 because negative charge means it gains one electron.

24. (A)

Electronic configuration of $_{12}Mg$ atom is = 2, 8, 2

Electronic configuration of Mg^{2+} ion is = 2, 8, because 2 positive charge means it loses two electrons.

HOTS (ACHIEVERS SECTION)

| 31. (C) | 32. (B) | 33. (B) | 34. (C) | 35. (A) |

5. CELL–THE FUNDAMENTAL UNIT OF LIFE

Answer Key

1. (C)	2. (B)	3. (A)	4. (A)	5. (C)	6.(A)	7. (C)	8 (B)	9. (B)	10. (B)
11. (C)	12. (A)	13. (D)	14. (A)	15. (D)	16. (D)	17. (A)	18. (C)	19. (B)	20. (C)
21. (B)	22. (C)	23. (C)	24. (D)	25. (C)	26. (C)	27. (B)	28. (C)	29. (A)	30. (D)

HOTS (ACHIEVERS SECTION)

| 31. (D) | 32. (B) | 33. (D) | 34. (C) | 35. (B) |

6. TISSUES

Answer Key

1. (B)	2. (C)	3. (B)	4. (C)	5. (B)	6.(C)	7. (C)	8. (A)	9. (A)	10. (C)
11. (B)	12. (C)	13. (B)	14. (D)	15. (C)	16. (C)	17. (B)	18. (A)	19. (C)	20. (A)
21. (B)	22. (C)	23. (B)	24. (A)	25. (C)	26. (C)	27. (C)	28. (A)	29. (A)	30. (A)

HOTS (ACHIEVERS SECTION)

| 31. (A) | 32. (B) | 33. (B) | 34. (D) | 35. (D) |

Answer Key

1. (B)	2. (A)	3. (D)	4. (C)	5. (B)	6. (C)	7. (A)	8. (A)	9. (C)	10. (B)
11. (A)	12. (C)	13. (B)	14. (C)	15. (B)	16. (B)	17. (A)	18. (D)	19. (D)	20. (B)
21. (C)	22. (B)	23. (A)	24. (C)	25. (A)	26. (C)	27. (D)	28. (B)	29. (C)	30. (A)

HOTS (ACHIEVERS SECTION)

31. (B)	32. (D)	33. (D)	34. (D)	35. (C)

8. MOTION

Answer Key

1. (A)	2. (B)	3. (C)	4. (A)	5. (B)	6. (D)	7. (C)	8. (D)	9. (B)	10. (C)
11. (A)	12. (C)	13. (B)	14. (B)	15. (D)	16. (A)	17. (A)	18. (B)	19. (C)	20. (B)
21. (A)	22. (B)	23. (B)	24. (B)	25. (C)	26. (A)	27. (C)	28. (C)	29. (B)	30. (D)

2. (B)

Distance travelled $= \dfrac{1}{2} \times$ Area of rectangle OQPR

$= \dfrac{1}{2} \times OR \times OQ$

OR = speed,
OQ = time at
OP → velocity curve.

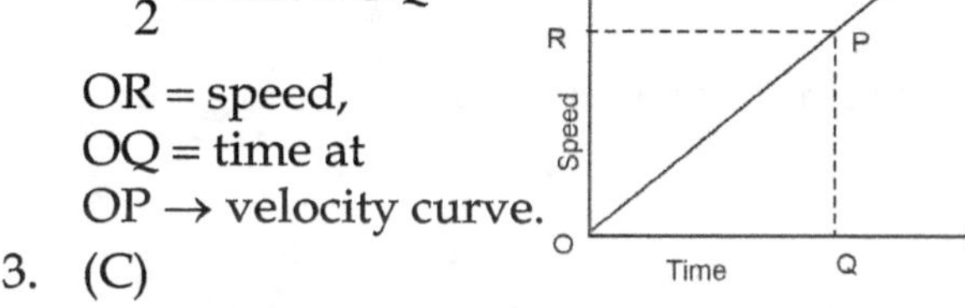

3. (C)

Applying Pythagoras theorem,

$OQ = \sqrt{OP^2 + PQ^2}$

$\qquad = \sqrt{36 + 64} = 10$

Since, OQ is the actual displacement.

4. (A)

A man starts from O and reaches Q. Shortest distance is OQ.

Apply Pythagoras theorem to $\triangle ORQ$.

(RQ = PM) and (PR = MQ)

$OQ^2 = OR^2 + RQ^2$

$= (2 + 6)^2 + (6)^2 = \sqrt{64 + 36}$

$OQ = \sqrt{100} = 10 \text{ m}$

5. (B)

As the direction keeps on changing continuously in a circular motion, the speed remains constant but velocity keeps on changing all the time.

6. (D)

$\text{Acceleration} = \dfrac{\text{change in velocity}}{\text{Time taken}}$

7. (C)

In case of speed-time graph, having a constant line parallel to time (x) axis, we see that speed is fixed (constant) but time keeps on moving in this graph as shown, Speed = u (throughout).

8. (D)

$\text{Speed} = \dfrac{\text{Distance}}{\text{Time}}$

t_1 for first 40 km $= \dfrac{d_1}{v_1} = \dfrac{40}{55} = \dfrac{8}{11} h$

t_2 for next 20 km $= \dfrac{d_2}{v_2} = \dfrac{20}{50} = \dfrac{2}{5}h$

Total time taken $= t_1 + t_2 = \dfrac{8}{11} + \dfrac{2}{5} = \dfrac{62}{55}h$

$$= 1.127 \text{ hours.}$$

12. (C)

$$A = \frac{v-u}{t} = \frac{45-30}{3} = 5 \text{ m/s}^2.$$

Here, acceleration, is positive as speed is increasing.

14. (B)

The line graph for car B makes a larger angle with time-axis. Its slope is larger than the slope of the line for car A. And the slope of distance-time graph shows speed. Thus car B has greater speed than car A.

15. (D)

$$v = 72 \text{ km/h} = 72 \times \frac{5}{18} = 20 \text{ m/s}$$

$$u = 36 \text{ km/h} = 36 \times \frac{5}{18} = 10 \text{ m/s}$$

$$t = 10 \text{ sec.}$$

$$A = \frac{v-u}{t} = \frac{20-10}{10} = 1 \text{ m/s}^2.$$

16. (A)

$$v = u + at$$
$$= 15 + 2.5 \times 2 = 20 \text{ m/s.}$$

17. (A)

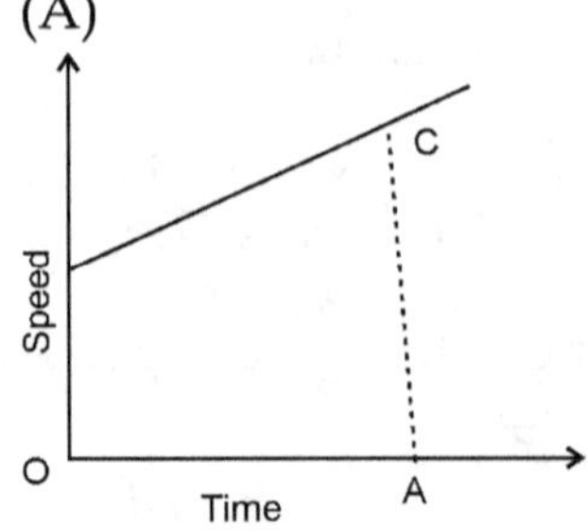

Area of trapezium $= \dfrac{(OB + AC) \times OA}{2}$

$=$ Distance travelled in A seconds, whose unit is m. Initial speed $=$ OB, then accelerating from B to C in time A.

19. (C)

Distance $= \dfrac{1}{2} \times$ base $\times$ height

$$= \frac{1}{2} \times 20 \text{ s} \times 20 \text{ m/s} = 200 \text{ m.}$$

20. (B)

Slope of the distance-time graph shows speed. The slope of line B is smallest, thus cyclist B is the slowest and cyclist C is the fastest among all four cyclists.

21. (A)

A horizontal line parallel to the time-axis shows a uniform velocity throughout the motion of the object.

22. (B)

When a body comes to rest, $v = 0$, here $u = 30$ m/s,

$a = -1.5$ m/s^2

$v = u + at$

$$t = \frac{v-u}{a} = \frac{0-30}{-1.5} = \frac{-30}{-1.5} = 20 \text{ seconds}$$

23. (B)

$u = 15$ km/h, $v = 60$ km/h, $t = 300$ sec $= \dfrac{1}{12}h$

$$a = \frac{v-u}{t} = \frac{60-15}{1/12} = 540 \text{ km/h}^2$$

Distance travelled by the car is given by

$$S = ut + \frac{1}{2}at^2$$

$$= 15 \times \frac{1}{12} + \frac{1}{2} \times 540 \times \frac{1}{12} \times \frac{1}{12}$$

$$= 3.1 \text{ km}$$

24. (B)

$v = 0$, $u = 20$ m/s, $t = 5$ s;

$$a = \frac{v-u}{t} = \frac{0-20}{5} - 4 \, m/s^2$$

25. (C)

$R = 32000$ km, $t = 30$ hours

Circumference of the orbit $= 2\pi R$

$$= 2 \times \frac{22}{7} \times 32000$$

$= 201{,}142.86 \text{ km}$

$\text{velocity} = \dfrac{d}{t} = \dfrac{2\pi R}{t} = \dfrac{201{,}142.86}{30} \approx 6704 \, km/h$

26. (A)

$v = \dfrac{2\pi r}{t} = \dfrac{2 \times \dfrac{22}{7} \times 45}{180} = 2 \times \dfrac{22}{7} \times \dfrac{45}{180} = \dfrac{11}{7} = 1.57 ms$

$t = 3, \ m = 180 \ \text{Sceonds}, \ r = 45 \text{ m}$

28. (C)

As we move along the graph, PQ and ST shows uniform acceleration. QR shows acceleration at an increasing rate. RS shows deceleration i.e., speed is decreasing.

30. (D)

$u = 0, \ v = 72 \text{ km/h} = 72 \times \dfrac{5}{18} = 20 \text{ ms}{-1},$

$t = 5 \text{ minutes} = 300 \text{ s}$

$a = \dfrac{v-u}{t} = \dfrac{20}{300} = \dfrac{1}{15} m/s^2$

$v^2 = u^2 + 2as$

$s = \dfrac{v^2 - u^2}{2a} = \dfrac{(20)^2 - (0)^2}{2 \times \dfrac{1}{15}} = 3000 \text{ m}$

$= 3 \text{ kms.}$

HOTS (ACHIEVERS SECTION)

31. (D)	32. (C)	33. (C)	34. (A)	35. (B)

9. FORCE AND LAWS OF MOTION

Answer Key

1. (B)	2. (D)	3. (A)	4. (C)	5. (C)	6. (C)	7. (A)	8. (B)	9. (A)	10. (C)
11. (C)	12. (D)	13. (B)	14. (C)	15. (A)	16. (B)	17. (A)	18. (D)	19. (D)	20. (C)
21. (A)	22. (C)	23. (D)	24. (C)	25. (A)	26. (C)	27. (B)	28. (C)	29. (B)	30. (A)

1. (B)

A lighter body accelerates more easily than a heavy body, thus mass is the factor whose SI unit is kg.

5. (C)

Momentum = mass × velocity

$\dfrac{\text{Change in momentum}}{\text{Time}} = \text{mass} \times \dfrac{\text{Change in velocity}}{\text{Time}}$

$= \text{mass} \times \text{acceleration}$

$= \text{Force}$

6. (C)

$F = ma \Rightarrow a = \dfrac{F}{m}$

If $F' \Rightarrow 2F$, and $m \Rightarrow 2m$,

new acceleration $a' = \dfrac{F'}{m'} = \dfrac{2F}{2m} = \dfrac{F}{m} = a$

Thus, acceleration remains the same.

8. (B)

As his weight (mass increases), his inertia will also increase.

9. (A)

$5 = M \times 10 \Rightarrow \quad M = 0.5 \text{ kg} \ (F = ma)$

$5 = m \times 20 \Rightarrow \quad m = 0.25 \text{ kg}$

$5 = (M + m) \times a \Rightarrow 5 = (0.5 + 0.25) \times a$

$\Rightarrow a = \dfrac{5}{0.75} = \dfrac{500}{75} = 6.6 \, ms^{-2}$

10. (C)

According to the Newton's third law, every action has an equal and opposite reaction.

12. (D)

If the two bodies stick to each other after collision, they will move with a common velocity v given by:

$$V = \frac{m_a\, u_a + m_b\, u_b}{m_a + m_b}$$

Here, $m_a = 20$ kg, $u_a = 2$ m/s, $m_b = 2$ kg, $u_b = 0$

$$\therefore\ v = \frac{20 \times 2 + 2 \times 0}{20 + 2} = \frac{40}{22} = 1.81 \text{ m/s}$$

13. (B)

$m_1 = 20$ g $= 0.02$ kg, $m_2 = 2$ kg.

$u_1 = 0$, $u_2 = 0$ (both pistol and bullet are at rest)

$v_1 = +150$ ms^{-1} (the find velocity of the bullet)

let v_2 be the recoil velocity of the pistol according to the law of conservation, total moment remains the same.

$m_1 u_1 + m_2 u_2 = m_1 v_1 + m_2 v_2$

$.02 \times 0 + 2 \times 0 = 0.02 \times 150 + 2 \times v_2$

$0 = 3 + 2v_2$

$$\Rightarrow v_2 = \frac{-3}{2} = -1.5 \text{ ms}^{-1}$$

Negative sign indicates that the pistol will recoil in the opposite direction of the bullet.

15. (A)

$$f = \frac{m(v-u)}{t} = 5\frac{(7-3)}{2} = 10\,N$$

16. (B)

$m_1 = 2$ kg, $a_1 = 5$ ms^{-2}, $m_2 = 4$ kg, $a_2 = 2$ ms^{-2}

$F_1 = m_1 a_1 = 10$ N, $F_2 = 4 \times 2 = 8$ N

$\Rightarrow F_1 > F_2$

Thus, a body of mass 2 kg requires more force to accelerate at 5 ms^{-2}.

18. (D)

No force is required as per the Newton's first law of motion.

20. (C)

impulse = force × time Ns

22. (C)

$F = 5$ N, $a_1 = 8$ ms^{-2}, $a_2 = 24$ ms^{-2}

$$\Rightarrow\ F = m_1 a_1 \Rightarrow m_1 = \frac{5}{8},\, f = m_2 a_2 \Rightarrow m_2 = \frac{5}{24}$$

For two bodies combined, $f = (m_1 + m_2)\, a$

$$m_1 + m_2 = \frac{5}{8} + \frac{5}{24} = \frac{20}{24} = \frac{5}{6} \text{ kg. } f = 5N$$

$$\therefore\ 5 = \frac{5}{6}a \Rightarrow a = 6 \text{ ms}^{-2}$$

23. (D)

For every force exerted on a body, equal and opposite force is exerted by other body on it to balance the body

24. (C)

The sports car has minimum weight,

$$F = ma \Rightarrow a = \frac{f}{m} \times \frac{1}{m}$$

Acceleration is maximum for the body with the least weight.

26. (C)

$F = m \times a$, $5 = 20 \times a \Rightarrow a = 0.25$ m/s^2

30. (A)

Change in momentum $= m \times (v - u)$

$= 10 \times (0.2 - 20)$

$= 10 \times (-19.8)$

$= -198$ Ns.

HOTS (ACHIEVERS SECTION)

31. (B)	32. (A)	33. (B)	34. (A)	35. (A)

Answer Key

1. (B)	2. (B)	3. (A)	4. (C)	5. (D)	6. (A)	7. (A)	8. (B)	9. (D)	10. (B)
11. (C)	12. (A)	13. (B)	14. (C)	15. (B)	16. (A)	17. (D)	18. (D)	19. (A)	20. (C)
21. (B)	22. (C)	23. (C)	24. (C)	25. (B)	26. (C)	27. (A)	28. (B)	29. (C)	30. (D)

1. **(B)**

   $$h = ut + \frac{1}{2}at^2$$

   Initial velocity, $u = 0$, $t = 0.5$ s, $a = 10$ ms^{-2}

   $$h = 0 \times 0.5 + \frac{1}{2} \times 10 \times \frac{1}{2} \times \frac{1}{2}$$

   $$= 1.25 \text{ m}$$

3. **(A)**

   The force of attraction F is inversely proportional to the square of distance between two objects. When distance is doubled, force becomes one-fourth.

4. **(C)**

   $$F = G\frac{m_1 m_2}{r^2}$$

6. **(A)**

   $$F = G \times \frac{mM}{r^2}$$

   $$= 6.67 \times 10^{-11} \times \frac{200 \times 800}{50 \times 50} = 4.26 \times 10^{-9}\,\text{N}$$

7. **(A)**

   Force of gravity is directed downwards, against the direction of the object going upward.

8. **(B)**

   $v = u + at$

   $u = 0$, $a = g = 9.8$ ms^2, $t = 2$ s

   $v = 2 \times 9.8 = 19.6$ ms^{-1}

9. **(D)**

   $v = u + at$

   $u = 19.6$, $a = g = -9.8$ m/s^2, $t = 5$ s

   $v = 19.6 + (-9.8) \times 3$

   $v = -9.8$ m/s

12. **(A)**

    When a moving body attains maximum height, final velocity becomes zero.

13. **(B)**

    $v^2 = u^2 + 2gh$, $u = 0$

    $$v = \frac{1}{6}$$

    $$\sqrt{2gh} = \sqrt{2 \times 9.8 \times 100} = \sqrt{1960} = 44.2 \text{ M/s}$$

14. **(C)**

    $$g = \frac{GM}{R^2} = \frac{6.7 \times 10^{-11} \times 7.4 \times 10^{22}}{(1.74 \times 10^6)^2}$$

    (R = 1740 km = 1740 × 1000 m = 1.74 × 106 m

    $$\Rightarrow g = 1.63 \text{ m/s}^2$$

15. **(B)**

    $u = ?$, $v = 0$, $g = -9.8$ m/s^2 as ball goes up,

    $h = 19.6$ m

    $v^2 = u^2 + 2gh$

    $0^2 = u^2 + 2(-9.8) \times 19.6$

    $\Rightarrow u^2 = (19.6)^2$

    $\Rightarrow u = 19.6$ m/s

16. **(A)**

    $$g_{moon} = \frac{1}{6}\,g_{earth}$$

    $$= \frac{1}{6} \times 10 = 1.66 \text{ m/s}^2$$

20. **(C)**

    At centre, $g = 0$

21. **(B)**

    $u = 15$, $v = 0$, $g = -9.8$

    $v^2 = u^2 + 2gh$

$$0^2 = (15)^2 + 2(-9.8)\,h$$

$$\Rightarrow \quad h = \frac{15 \times 15}{2 \times 9.8} = \frac{225}{19.6} = 11.4\,m$$

22. (C)

$$g_{moon} = \frac{1}{6}\,g_{earth}$$

$$\therefore \quad W_{moon} = \frac{1}{6}\,W_{earth} = \frac{1}{6} \times 120 = 20\,kg$$

23. (C)

When breadth and height form the base, wooden block is standing vertically on the ground, exerting maximum pressure due to minimum area covered.

l = 50, b = 25, h = 10

Area 1 = l × b = 1250 cm²

Area 2 = l × h = 50 × 10 = 500 cm²

Area 3 = b × h = 25 × 10 = 250 cm²

Area 3 is the minimum, and pressure = $\dfrac{\text{Force}}{\text{Area}}$

24. (C)

Relative density of iron is 7.8 and that of mercury is 13.6. Thus, mercury is heavier than iron.

25. (B)

According to the Archimedes' principle the buoyant force acting on this ball B will be equal to the weight of water displaced by this ball. Weight = m × g and m = volume × density

∴ Ball b has maximum volume of liquid (24 mL) displaced .

27. (A)

The weight of liquid displaced = loss in weight

= 10N - 8N

= 2N

28. (B)

Weight = mg

m = 120 kg g on moon = $\dfrac{1}{6} \times$ g on the earth

$$= \frac{1}{6} \times 9.8$$

$$\therefore \quad \text{weight} = 120 \times \frac{1}{6} \times 9.8 = 2 \times 98 = 196\,N$$

30. (D)

Relative density is purely a ratio of two similar quantities (masses), so it has no units.

HOTS (ACHIEVERS SECTION)

31. (B)	32. (C)	33. (B)	34. (B)	35. (C)

11. WORK AND ENERGY

Answer Key

1. (B)	2. (B)	3. (A)	4. (A)	5. (C)	6. (B)	7. (A)	8. (C)	9. (B)	10. (A)
11. (C)	12. (B)	13. (A)	14. (D)	15. (D)	16. (C)	17. (A)	18. (D)	19. (D)	20. (B)
21. (A)	22. (D)	23. (B)	24. (C)	25. (C)	26. (C)	27. (B)	28. (C)	29. (D)	30. (B)

1. (B)

W = mgh

$= 50 \times 10 \times \dfrac{200}{100} = 1000$ J

2. (B)

When the displacement of a body is perpendicular (at 90°) to the direction of force (gravitational weight mg in this case), no work is done.

W = F cosθ × s

= F × cos90° × s

= 0 (cos 90° = 0)

3. (A)

W = f cos60° × d

$= 15 \times \dfrac{1}{2} \times 20$

= 150 Nm = 150 J

5. (C)

K.E. $= \dfrac{1}{2}$ mv² $= \dfrac{1}{2} \times 0.1 \times 0.1 \times 2$

= 0.01 J

6. (B)

P.E. = mgh

480 j = 12 kg × 10 ms⁻² × h

h $= \dfrac{480\,\text{J}}{120\,\text{kg}\,\text{ms}^{-2}}$ = 4 m

The object is at the height of 4 m above the ground.

7. (A)

K.E. $= \dfrac{1}{2} mv^2$

$p = mv \Rightarrow$ K.E. $= \dfrac{1}{2} m \left(\dfrac{p}{m}\right)^2 = \dfrac{p^2}{2m}$

$\therefore \ \dfrac{\text{K.E}_1}{\text{K.E}_2} = \dfrac{p_1^2/2m_1}{p_2^2/2m_2} = \dfrac{m_2}{m_1} = \dfrac{p_1^2}{p_2^2}$

Here 'p_1' = p_2 (given)

$\therefore \ \dfrac{\text{K.E}_1}{\text{K.E}_2} = \dfrac{4 \times 10^{-3}\,\text{kg}}{1 \times 10^{-3}\,\text{kg}} = \dfrac{4}{1}$

9. (B)

P.E. = mgh

$= 100 \text{ kg} \times 10 \text{ m/s}^2 \times \dfrac{50}{100}\text{m}$

= 500 J

11. (C)

Energy due to motion = K.E. $= \dfrac{1}{2}$ mv²

$= \dfrac{1}{2} \times \dfrac{550}{1000}\,\text{kg} \times (25\text{m}/\text{sec})^2$

= 171.875 J

12. (B)

K.E. $= \dfrac{1}{2}mv^2 = \dfrac{1}{2} \times \left(\dfrac{250}{1000}\right) \times (10)^2 = 12.5\,j$

13. (A)

Both the spheres are under the force of gravity (g = a)

14. (D)

K.E. $= \dfrac{1}{2}$ mv²

$V = \sqrt{\dfrac{2\text{K.E}}{m}} = \sqrt{\dfrac{2 \times 1^2}{1}} = \sqrt{2} = 1.4\,\text{m/s}$

17. (A)

Potential energy is due to its position and not motion

19. (D)

W = F cosθ × s

For, θ = 180°, cosθ = -1

Force acts in opposite direction of the motion of the body

20. (B)

K.E. $= \dfrac{1}{2} mv^2 = \dfrac{1}{2}\dfrac{(mv)^2}{m} = \dfrac{p^2}{2m}$

(p = 2m = momentum)

Here $p_h = p_l$ of the two unequal masses m_e and m_h

$\dfrac{\text{K.E}_h}{\text{K.E}_L} = \dfrac{m_1}{m_h} \Rightarrow \text{K.E}_h = \dfrac{m_e}{w_h}(\text{K.E}_l)$

$\therefore$ K.Eh < K.E$_l$

21. (A)

Momentum, P.E. and K.E. are directly dependent on the mass of the body. So for two bodies of different masses, these three measures can never be same. Both the freely falling balls are under the same acceleration i.e., gravity g.

22. (D)

$w = F\cos\theta \times s$

23. (B)

$P = 60$ W

$\quad = 0.06$ kW

Time, $t = 6$ h

Energy $=$ power $\times$ time

$\quad = 0.06$ kW $\times 6$ h

$\quad = 0.36$ kWh

$\quad = 0.36$ 'units'

25. (C)

$$\text{K.E.} = \frac{1}{2}mv^2 = \frac{p^2}{2m} \quad (m = 20 \text{ g} = 0.02 \text{ kg})$$

$$= \frac{10\times10}{2\times0.02} = 2500 \text{ j} = 2.5 \text{ kj}$$

29. (D)

$Mg = 400$ N, $h = 2$ m

$\therefore$ work done $=$ P.E. $=$ mgh $= 800$ Nm $= 800$ J

HOTS (ACHIEVERS SECTION)				
31. (B)	32. (B)	33. (D)	34. (C)	35. (A)

12. SOUND

Answer Key

1. (B)	2. (B)	3. (C)	4. (B)	5. (C)	6. (B)	7.(B)	8 (A)	9. (A)	10. (C)
11. (D)	12. (B)	13. (A)	14. (B)	15. (A)	16. (C)	17. (A)	18. (A)	19. (B)	20. (A)
21. (C)	22. (A)	23. (D)	24. (A)	25. (B)					

4. (B)

$$= \frac{2}{\;} = \frac{2\times480}{\;}$$

$$= 480 \text{ ms}^{-1}$$

5. (C)

$v = v\lambda$

$$\lambda = \frac{340}{1.700} = .2 \text{ m or } 20 \text{ cm}$$

8. (A)

$$v = \frac{2d}{t} \text{ or } t = \frac{2d}{v}$$

$$= \frac{2\times660}{330} = 4\text{s}$$

14. (B)

$$T = \frac{1}{v} = \frac{1}{25}$$

$$= .04 \text{ sec.}$$

15. (A)

$$V = \frac{2d}{t} \text{ or } d = \frac{v\times t}{2}$$

$$= \frac{1450\times4}{2} = 2900 \text{ m or } 2.9 \text{ km.}$$

23. (D)

$$V = \frac{2d}{t} \text{ or } d = \frac{v\times t}{2}$$

$$= \frac{1500\times.4}{2} = 300 \text{ m}$$

HOTS (ACHIEVERS SECTION)

| 26. (C) | 27. (A) | 28. (C) | 29. (D) | 30. (B) |

13. WHY DO WE FALL ILL

Answer Key

1. (D)	2. (B)	3. (A)	4. (B)	5. (C)	6. (D)	7. (D)	8. (A)	9. (B)	10. (B)
11. (C)	12. (B)	13. (A)	14. (D)	15. (A)	16. (C)	17. (B)	18. (A)	19. (B)	20. (C)
21. (B)	22. (A)	23. (C)	24. (D)	25. (B)	26. (D)	27. (B)	28. (C)	29. (D)	30. (B)

HOTS (ACHIEVERS SECTION)

31. (A)	32. (B)	33. (B)	34. (C)	35. (D)

14. NATURAL RESOURCES

Answer Key

1. (C)	2. (B)	3. (B)	4. (D)	5. (B)	6. (A)	7. (A)	8. (D)	9. (D)	10. (B)
11. (B)	12. (D)	13. (C)	14. (B)	15. (C)	16. (A)	17. (C)	18. (B)	19. (B)	20. (C)
21. (C)	22. (A)	23. (B)	24. (A)	25. (C)	26. (B)	27. (B)	28. (C)	29. (D)	30. (C)

HOTS (ACHIEVERS SECTION)

31. (D)	32. (A)	33. (B)	34. (D)	35. (B)

32. (A)

Deforestation and greenhouse gases like carbon dioxide and CH4 that are released into the air from factories cause greenhouse effect.

33. (B)

In the given figure arrow labelled R represents photosynthesis, P represents respiration and Q represents combustion.

34. (C)

The option R represents decomposition by micro-organisms and S represents nitrogen fixation.

35. (A)

In the given figure X is respiration Y is photosynthesis, and Z is decomposition.

15. IMPROVEMENT IN FOOD RESOURCES

Answer Key

1. (C)	2. (B)	3. (D)	4. (A)	5. (A)	6. (B)	7. (A)	8.(B)	9. (D)	10 (A)
11. (B)	12. (A)	13. (B)	14. (D)	15. (A)	16. (C)	17. (B)	18. (D)	19. (B)	20. (C)
21. (D)	22. (C)	23. (D)	24. (C)	25. (A)	26. (A)	27. (B)	28. (C)	29. (B)	30. (D)

31. (A)	32. (D)	33. (C)	34. (B)	35. (D)

31. (A)
Rinderpest and haemorrhagic septicemia are diseases of cattle and ranikhet is a poultry disease.

33. (C)
Bee wax is secretion of worker bees abdominal glands. Sahiwal cow and Murrah buffalo are indigenous breeds of cattle, not exotic.

34. (B)
Kharif crops are those crops that are grown in rainy season from June to October, e.g., paddy: soybean, maize and cotton. Fodder crops are those crops that are grown as food for the livestock, e.g. berseem, sorghum, etc. Out of the seventeen nutrient elements required by plants, nine are required in. larger amounts, these are called macronutrients e.g., carbon, hydrogen, oxygen, nitrogen, phosphorus, potassium, calcium, magnesium and sulphur.

16. LOGICAL REASONING

Answer Key

1. (B)	2. (C)	3. (D)	4. (B)	5. (A)	6. (C)	7. (C)	8. (D)	9. (A)	10. (C)
11. (B)	12. (D)	13. (C)	14. (C)	15. (C)	16. (C)	17. (A)	18. (B)	19. (B)	20. (D)
21. (B)	22. (B)	23. (D)	24. (C)	25. (B)	26. (A)	27. (D)	28. (C)	29. (C)	30. (A)
31. (B)	32. (B)	33. (C)	34. (A)	35. (B)	36. (B)	37. (A)	38. (A)	39. (C)	40. (B)
41. (A)	42. (C)	43. (E)	44. (E)	45. (A)	46. (C)	47. (C)	48. (D)	49. (B)	50. (C)
51. (A)	52. (B)	53. (C)	54. (A)	55. (D)	56. (C)	57. (C)	58. (A)	59. (B)	60. (C)

1. (B)
First word is hatred for the second word.

2. (C)
The word in each pair are synonyms of each other.

3. (D)
The second word is more intense form of first word.

4. (B)
Money paid for accommodation is called rent. Money paid for travel is called fare.

5. (A)
Except pallete, all words are parts of a gun.

6. (C)
Except explosion, all words are natural calamites.

7. (C)
Except Groundnut, all are types of spices.

8. (D)
Bunker is related to Polo, but all others are related to Hockey.

9. (A)
The given numbers are in the set of three numbers which are pythagorian triplet.
$3^2 + 4^2 = 5^2$, $5^2 + 12^2 = 13^2$,
$7^2 + 24^2 = 25^2$, $9^2 + 40^2 = 41^2$.

10. (C)
The pattern of the given series is:
$3 - 1 = 2$; $6 - 3 = 3$; $10 - 6 = 4$;

$15 - 10 = 5; \ 21 - 15 = 6;$

$\therefore \quad 21 + 7 = 28$

11. (B)

The pattern of the given series is

$32 + 1 = 10; \ 42 + 1 = 17; \ 52 + 1 = 26;$

$62 + 1 = 37; \ 72 + 1 = 50;$

$\therefore \quad 8^2 + 1 = 65$

12. (D)

Here

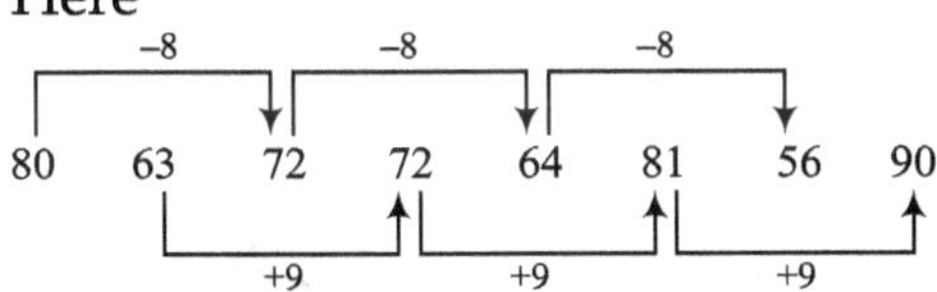

$\therefore \quad ? = 90$

13. (C)

Taking, $Z = 2, Y = 3, \ldots\ldots N = 14,$

$\qquad B = 26, A = 27$

$\therefore \quad ZIP = (2 + 19 + 12) \times 6 = 33 \times 6 = 198$

and $VIP = (V + I + P) \times 6 = (6 + 19 + 12) \times 6$

$\qquad\qquad = 37 \times 6 = 222$

Hence, $ZAP = (Z + A + P) \times 6$

$\qquad\qquad = (2 + 27 + 12) \times 6$

$\qquad\qquad = 41 \times 6 = 246$

14. (C)

Here, STATEMENT $\rightarrow$ TNEMETATS

Then, POLITICAL $\rightarrow$ LACITILOP

15. (C) Given, $134 \rightarrow$ good and tasty.

$\qquad\qquad 478 \rightarrow$ see good pictures

$\qquad\qquad 728 \rightarrow$ pictures are faint.

Hence, $4 \rightarrow$ Good and $8 \rightarrow$ Pictures

16. (C)

Here, it be pee $\rightarrow$ roses are blue

$\qquad\qquad$ sik hee $\rightarrow$ red flowers

$\qquad\qquad$ pee mit hee $\rightarrow$ flowers are vegetables

$\therefore \quad$ Hee $\rightarrow$ flowers, sik $\rightarrow$ red

17. (A)

When Pankaj shifts 3 places towards Raju his position is 15th from right and 10th from left.

$\therefore \quad$ No. of students $= 15 + 10 - 1 = 24$ students.

18. (B)

Day after tomorrow is Saturday, means today is Thursday. Yesterday was Wednesday, three days before Wednesday was Sunday.

19. (B)

1st November is Wednesday.

31st October is Tuesday.

29th, 22th, 15th, 8th, 1st October was Sunday.

20. (D)

January 2008 = 6 days

February 2008 = 29 days

March 2008 = 31 days

April 2008 = 30 days

May 2008 = 15 days

Total number of days from 26th January 2008 to 15th May 2008

$= 6 + 29 + 31 + 30 + 15 = 111$ days

21. (B)

As per question

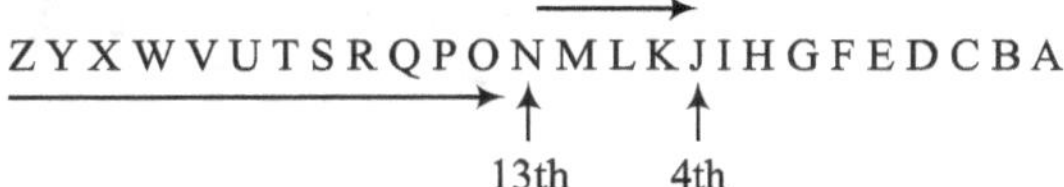

$\therefore \quad$ J is required latter.

22. (B)

A B C D P O N M L K J I H G F E Q R S T U V W X Y Z

$\qquad$ 7th $\qquad\qquad$ 14th

23. (D)

According to the question AZ, BY, CX, DW, EV, FU, GT, HS, IR, JQ, KP, LO, MN.

24. (C)

According to the question

Z Y X W V U T S R Q P O N M L K J I H G F E D C B A

$\qquad\qquad\qquad$ 8th

25. (B)

Meena's mother's son = Meena's brother

Rajan is son of Meena's brother.

So, Meena is Rajan's aunt.

26. (A)

Sarita's father's only daughter means Sarita.

Rekha is Sarita's daughter.

27. (D)

Sulekha's father's only son = Sulekha's brother

Kanchan is son of Sulekha's brother.

Kanchan's mother is wife of Sulekha's brother.

So, Kanchan's mother is Sulekha's sister-in-law.

28. (C)

Daughter of grandmother = Aunt

Aunt's only brother = father

29. (C)

We have, $4 \, P \, 10 \, Q \, 6 \, R \, 3 \, S \, 8$

$$= 4 + 10 \times 6 \div 3 - 8$$
$$= 4 + 10 \times 2 - 8$$
$$= 4 + 20 - 8$$
$$= 24 - 8 = 16$$

30. (A)

Here, $14 \, A \, 6 \, B \, 8 \, C \, 2 \, D \, 12$

$$= 14 \times 6 + 8 \div 2 - 12$$
$$= 14 \times 6 + 4 - 12$$
$$= 84 + 4 - 12$$
$$= 88 - 12 = 76$$

31. (B)

Here, $27 \, J \, 15 \, K \, 2 \, M \, 18 \, L \, 3$

$$= 27 - 15 \times 2 + 18 \div 3$$
$$= 27 - 15 \times 2 + 6$$
$$= 27 - 30 + 6$$
$$= 33 - 30 = 3$$

32. (B)

(A) $15 - 5 \div 5 \times 20 + 10 = 6$
$$15 \times 5 + 5 - 20 \div 10 = 6$$
$$15 \times 5 + 5 - 2 = 6$$
$$78 \neq 6$$

(B) $8 \div 10 - 3 + 5 \times 6 = 8$
$$8 + 10 \times 3 \div 5 - 6 = 8$$
$$8 + 10 \times \frac{3}{5} - 6 = 8$$
$$8 + 6 - 6 = 8$$
$$8 = 8$$

Hence, (B) is true.

33. (C)

Let the no. of horses = x

No. of men = x

$\therefore$ total number of legs $= 4x + 2 \times \dfrac{x}{2} = 70$

$$\Rightarrow \quad 5x = 70 \qquad\qquad \Rightarrow x = 14$$

34. (A)

Let Ram's age = x, Mohan's age = y

Lokesh's age = z

$\therefore \qquad\qquad x = 3y \qquad\qquad$ ...(i)

and $\qquad z - 4 = 2 \, (x - 4)$

$$z = 2x - 8 + 4 = 2x - 4 \qquad ...(ii)$$
$$+ 4 = 31 \Rightarrow x = 27$$
$$3y = 27 \Rightarrow y = 9$$

Using eqn. (ii) $z = 2x - 4 = 2 \times 27 - 4 = 50$

Hence, $\qquad z - y = 50 - 9 = 41$

35. (B)

Let Mukesh's today age = x years.

$\therefore \quad x + 1 = 2 \, (x - 12)$

$$x + 1 = 2x - 24$$
$$\Rightarrow \qquad x = 25 \text{ years}$$

36. (B)

Let Rajesh solves x sums correctly.

Right sums = x, wrong sums = $2x$

$\therefore \qquad\quad x + 2x = 84$

$$\Rightarrow \qquad\qquad 3x = 84$$
$$\Rightarrow \qquad\qquad x = 28$$

37. (A)

Here, $\left(\sqrt{1} + \sqrt{9} + \sqrt{25} + \sqrt{81} \right)^2$

$$= (1 + 3 + 5 + 9)2 = (18)2 = 324$$

and $\left(\sqrt{64} + \sqrt{4} + \sqrt{9} + \sqrt{16} \right)^2$

$$= (8 + 2 + 3 + 4)2 = (17)2 = 289$$

$\therefore \quad ? = \left(\sqrt{16} + \sqrt{25} + \sqrt{1} + \sqrt{81} \right)^2$

$$= (4 + 5 + 1 + 9)2 = 361$$

38. (A)

Here, $4 \times 2 \times 8 \times 6 = 384$

$$3 \times 3 \times 4 \times 6 = 216$$

$\therefore \qquad 6 \times 8 \times 7 \times 4 = 1344$

39. (C)

Here, $(3^2 + 6^2) - (2^2 + 4^2) = 45 - 20 = 25$

and $(11^2 + 7^2) - (6^2 + 8^2) = 170 - 100 = 70$

$\therefore \quad (x^2 + 3^2) - (2^2 + 7^2) = x^2 + 9 - 53 = 20$

$$= x^2 - 44 = 20$$
$$= x^2 = 64 \qquad \Rightarrow x = 8$$

40. (B)

Here, $(17 - 5) \times (2 + 7) = 12 \times 9 = 108$
and $(7 - 3) \times (8 + 3) = 4 \times 11 = 44$
$\therefore \ ? = (9 - 4) \times (7 + 8) = 5 \times 15 = 75$

41. (A)

Two and three half-leaves are added to the figure alternately. The addition of half-leaves takes place in an ACW direction.

42. (C)

The two elements together move two spaces (each space is equal to half-a-side of the square boundary) and three space ACW alternately. Also, in one step, the two elements interchange positions and together rotate 90° CW and in the next step, the two elements interchange their positions and together rotate through 180°.

43. (E)

The arrow moves one, two, three, four, ... spaces ACW sequentially. The arrowhead changes in the sequence: circle → arc → triangle → circle → ....

44. (E)

Five line segments are added in each step to complete the squares in an ACW direction.

57. (C)

In this figure, there is 1 column having 3 cubes, 7 columns containing 2 cubes and 13 columns containing 1 cube.

$\therefore$ Total number of cubes
$= 1 \times 3 + 7 \times 2 + 13 \times 1$
$= 3 + 14 + 13 = 30$

58. (A)

In this figure, there are 23 columns having 3 cubes each, 8 columns having 2 cubes each and 4 columns having 1 cube each.

$\therefore$ Total no. of cubes $= 23 \times 3 + 8 \times 2 + 4 \times 1$
$= 69 + 16 + 4 = 89$

59. (B)

In the figure, there are 48 colums having 3 cubes each and 12 columns having 2 cubes each.

$\therefore$ Total no. of cubes $= 48 \times 3 + 12 \times 2$
$= 144 + 24 = 168$

60. (C)

In this figure there are 11 columns having 4 cubes each, 7 columns having 3 cubes each and 2 columns having 2 cubes each.

$\therefore$ Total no. of cubes $= 11 \times 4 + 7 \times 3 + 2 \times 2$
$= 44 + 21 + 4 = 69$

MODEL TEST PAPER

Answer Key

1. (A)	2. (C)	3. (B)	4. (C)	5. (B)	6. (B)	7. (A)	8. (C)	9. (B)	10. (A)
11. (A)	12. (C)	13. (A)	14. (B)	15. (D)	16. (D)	17. (B)	18. (C)	19. (A)	20. (A)
21. (A)	22. (B)	23. (A)	24. (D)	25. (D)	26. (D)	27. (D)	28. (D)	29. (B)	30. (D)
31. (D)	32. (D)	33. (D)	34. (A)	35. (A)	36. (A)	37. (B)	38. (A)	39. (C)	40. (C)
41. (A)	42. (C)	43. (B)	44. (A)	45. (B)	46. (C)	47. (D)	48. (C)	49. (B)	50. (D)

SAMPLE OMR ANSWER SHEET

1. STUDENT NAME (IN ENGLISH CAPITAL LETTERS ONLY)

Students must write and darken the respective circles completely using HB Pencil only. Othewise their Answer Sheets will not be evaluated.

PERSONAL DETAILS

2. SCHOOL CODE

3. CLASS

4. SECTION

5. ROLL NO.

6. QUESTION PAPER SET

A ○
B ○
C ○
D ○

7. MOBILE NUMBER

8. GENDER

MALE ○
FEMALE ○

9. STREAM
(Only for Class XI and XII Students)

MATHEMATICS ○
BIOLOGY ○
OTHERS ○

MARK YOUR ANSWERS

	A	B	C	D		A	B	C	D
1.	Ⓐ	Ⓑ	Ⓒ	Ⓓ	26.	Ⓐ	Ⓑ	Ⓒ	Ⓓ
2.	Ⓐ	Ⓑ	Ⓒ	Ⓓ	27.	Ⓐ	Ⓑ	Ⓒ	Ⓓ
3.	Ⓐ	Ⓑ	Ⓒ	Ⓓ	28.	Ⓐ	Ⓑ	Ⓒ	Ⓓ
4.	Ⓐ	Ⓑ	Ⓒ	Ⓓ	29.	Ⓐ	Ⓑ	Ⓒ	Ⓓ
5.	Ⓐ	Ⓑ	Ⓒ	Ⓓ	30.	Ⓐ	Ⓑ	Ⓒ	Ⓓ
6.	Ⓐ	Ⓑ	Ⓒ	Ⓓ	31.	Ⓐ	Ⓑ	Ⓒ	Ⓓ
7.	Ⓐ	Ⓑ	Ⓒ	Ⓓ	32.	Ⓐ	Ⓑ	Ⓒ	Ⓓ
8.	Ⓐ	Ⓑ	Ⓒ	Ⓓ	33.	Ⓐ	Ⓑ	Ⓒ	Ⓓ
9.	Ⓐ	Ⓑ	Ⓒ	Ⓓ	34.	Ⓐ	Ⓑ	Ⓒ	Ⓓ
10.	Ⓐ	Ⓑ	Ⓒ	Ⓓ	35.	Ⓐ	Ⓑ	Ⓒ	Ⓓ
11.	Ⓐ	Ⓑ	Ⓒ	Ⓓ	36.	Ⓐ	Ⓑ	Ⓒ	Ⓓ
12.	Ⓐ	Ⓑ	Ⓒ	Ⓓ	37.	Ⓐ	Ⓑ	Ⓒ	Ⓓ
13.	Ⓐ	Ⓑ	Ⓒ	Ⓓ	38.	Ⓐ	Ⓑ	Ⓒ	Ⓓ
14.	Ⓐ	Ⓑ	Ⓒ	Ⓓ	39.	Ⓐ	Ⓑ	Ⓒ	Ⓓ
15.	Ⓐ	Ⓑ	Ⓒ	Ⓓ	40.	Ⓐ	Ⓑ	Ⓒ	Ⓓ
16.	Ⓐ	Ⓑ	Ⓒ	Ⓓ	41.	Ⓐ	Ⓑ	Ⓒ	Ⓓ
17.	Ⓐ	Ⓑ	Ⓒ	Ⓓ	42.	Ⓐ	Ⓑ	Ⓒ	Ⓓ
18.	Ⓐ	Ⓑ	Ⓒ	Ⓓ	43.	Ⓐ	Ⓑ	Ⓒ	Ⓓ
19.	Ⓐ	Ⓑ	Ⓒ	Ⓓ	44.	Ⓐ	Ⓑ	Ⓒ	Ⓓ
20.	Ⓐ	Ⓑ	Ⓒ	Ⓓ	45.	Ⓐ	Ⓑ	Ⓒ	Ⓓ
21.	Ⓐ	Ⓑ	Ⓒ	Ⓓ	46.	Ⓐ	Ⓑ	Ⓒ	Ⓓ
22.	Ⓐ	Ⓑ	Ⓒ	Ⓓ	47.	Ⓐ	Ⓑ	Ⓒ	Ⓓ
23.	Ⓐ	Ⓑ	Ⓒ	Ⓓ	48.	Ⓐ	Ⓑ	Ⓒ	Ⓓ
24.	Ⓐ	Ⓑ	Ⓒ	Ⓓ	49.	Ⓐ	Ⓑ	Ⓒ	Ⓓ
25.	Ⓐ	Ⓑ	Ⓒ	Ⓓ	50.	Ⓐ	Ⓑ	Ⓒ	Ⓓ

Signature of the Student & Date of Examination

Signature of the Invigilator & Date of Examination